WHEN FAITH MEETS CAPACITY

Miracles Happen When Divine Instruction Meets Human Preparation

Dr. Jean Héder Petit-Frère

When Faith Meets Capacity:
Miracles Happen When Divine Instruction Meets Human Preparation
Copyright © 2025 by Dr. Jean Héder Petit-Frère

All rights reserved.
No part of this publication may be reproduced, stored in a retrieval system, or transmitted in any form or by any means—electronic, mechanical, photocopying, recording, or otherwise—without the prior written permission of the author, except in the case of brief quotations embodied in critical articles or reviews.

All Scripture quotations, unless otherwise indicated, are taken from the New King James Version®, copyright © 1982 by Thomas Nelson. Used by permission. All rights reserved.

Scripture quotations marked ESV are taken from the *Holy Bible, English Standard Version*®, copyright © 2001 by Crossway, a publishing ministry of Good News Publishers. Used by permission. All rights reserved.

Scripture quotations marked NIV are taken from the *Holy Bible, New International Version*®, copyright © 1973, 1978, 1984, 2011 by Biblica, Inc.™ Used by permission. All rights reserved worldwide.

Edited and compiled in collaboration with:
Jean Héder Petit-Frère International

For more resources, teachings, and Kingdom training, visit: www.jhpetitfrere.com

All rights reserved worldwide.

Table of Content

ACKNOWLEDGMENTS PAGE — 7

FOREWORD — 9

INTRODUCTION

WHEN FAITH MEETS CAPACITY — 11

CHAPTER 1 — 15

THE WIDOW'S SECRET: FAITH IN CRISIS — 15

CHAPTER 2 — 21

THE TWO QUESTIONS THAT CHANGE YOUR DESTINY — 21

CHAPTER 3 — 27

THE POWER OF A "BUT" — 27

CHAPTER 4 — 33

THE OIL IN YOUR HOUSE — 33

CHAPTER 5 — 39

DISCOVER YOUR OIL — 39

CHAPTER 6 — 47

BORROWING CAPACITY: SYSTEMS, STRUCTURES, AND
MENTORS 47

CHAPTER 7 55

BORROWING VESSELS WELL 55

CHAPTER 8 61

SHUTTING THE DOOR: PRIVATE OBEDIENCE 61

CHAPTER 9 69

POUR UNTIL IT STOPS: THE LAW OF DIVINE MULTIPLICATION 69

CHAPTER 10 75

KINGDOM ECONOMICS: SELL THE OIL 75

CHAPTER 11 81

THE LIMIT OF OIL IS THE LIMIT OF VESSELS 81

CHAPTER 12 87

FAITH FOR HEAVEN, CAPACITY FOR EARTH 87

CHAPTER 13 95

BREAKING THE POVERTY MINDSET 95

CHAPTER 14 103

THE CAPACITY OF VISION	103
CHAPTER 15	111
PREPARING FOR THE OIL OF TOMORROW	111
CHAPTER 16	119
FAITH + CAPACITY IN MINISTRY, MARRIAGE, MONEY, AND LEADERSHIP	119
CHAPTER 17	127
LIVING A LIFE GOD CAN FILL	127
CONCLUSION	135
WHEN FAITH MEETS CAPACITY	135
THIS IS YOUR INVITATION	141
21-DAY ACTIVATION GUIDE	143

ACKNOWLEDGMENTS PAGE

Writing a book is an act of obedience, but producing a book is an act of community.
No assignment of this magnitude is ever walked alone, and I am grateful for every hand, every voice, and every heart that contributed to this journey.

My spiritual family and the global body of believers continually draw from the grace that God has placed on my life—your hunger pulls revelation from heaven. Thank you for valuing the message of the Kingdom and for positioning yourselves to grow.

To the faithful leaders, pastors, and servants who collaborate with me in many countries, your dedication inspires me. Your dedication to transformation strengthens my resolve to write, teach, build, and serve with excellence.

To all who encourage, pray, support, and believe in the vision God entrusted to me—your partnership makes it possible to continue reaching lives, shaping destinies, and expanding the Kingdom.

To every reader who will pick up this book with expectation and hope—thank you.
You are the reason this message was written.
May these pages become oil for your journey and vessels for your future.

Above all, to the Holy Spirit—my teacher, counselor, and constant source.

Thank you for revelation, for inspiration, and for the grace to write what you breathe.

All glory to the King.

FOREWORD

by: H.E. RT HON Dr. Phillip Phinn

There are books we read… and there are books that read us.

This is one of those rare works.

In "When Faith Meets Capacity," Dr. Jean Héder Petit-Frère addresses one of the most misunderstood dynamics in the Kingdom of God: the partnership between divine instruction and human preparation.

This book is not merely a commentary on 2 Kings 4; it is a prophetic blueprint for how God transforms a life, a family, a ministry, and a generation. Using the journey of the widow, Dr. Heder brings us into the tension between desperation and destiny, showing us that miracles are not random events — they are the result of alignment, obedience, capacity, and revelation.

What I appreciate most is that this book does not romanticize miracles. It shows us that faith alone is not enough. God always fills according to capacity. The oil does not stop because God is unwilling — it stops because the vessel is full. This single revelation, expressed with clarity and prophetic weight, has the power to reposition any believer.

Dr. Heder writes as a pastor, a teacher, a prophet, and an apostolic voice for this generation. His insights on emotional blindness, trauma, pressure, and comparison are both psychologically sound and spiritually piercing. His teaching on systems, vessels, and structure is deeply practical. And his revelation on Kingdom economics — "sell the oil and live of the rest" — is profoundly needed in the Body of Christ today.

If you have ever felt stuck, empty, inadequate, overlooked, or uncertain about your next step, read this book slowly. Read it prayerfully. Read it with expectation. Within these pages is a map — a Kingdom technology — for moving from limitation to multiplication.

It is my honor to commend this work to every believer, leader, and visionary who desires to live a life God can fill.

H.E. RT HON Dr. Phillip Phinn, DCPC, OEA
WOLMI President General
Chief Ambassador to the United Nations

INTRODUCTION

WHEN FAITH MEETS CAPACITY

"According to your faith be it unto you." (Matthew 9:29)
"Gather vessels—and not a few." (2 Kings 4:3)

There is a moment in every believer's life where faith alone is no longer the issue. The question is no longer, "Can *God do it?*" The question becomes: "Do I have the capacity to receive what He is ready to pour?"

This book was born from that revelation.

For years, I watched people pray sincerely, worship passionately, fast faithfully, and believe God wholeheartedly—yet remain stuck, limited, overwhelmed, or underdeveloped. This was not due to a lack of response from God, but rather a lack of space to hold the abundance He was bestowing upon them.

The widow in 2 Kings 4 embodies this tension beautifully. Her faith was real. Her desperation was real. Her pain was real. Her need was undeniable.

But her miracle did not begin with heaven, sending something new. It began when the prophet asked her a simple, destiny-altering question:

"What do you have in your house?"

The oil was already there. The capacity was not.

This book is written for anyone who has ever believed God for more but felt stuck in less. For every dreamer struggling with systems, structures, or support. For every believer who has prayed for increase but lived with internal limitations. For every called leader who carries anointing but lacks alignment. For every person who knows there is oil in their life—but does not yet know how to multiply it.

Here, you will discover that:

- Faith opens the door, but capacity sustains the blessing.
- Anointing unlocks possibilities, but structure unlocks longevity.
- Miracles begin with what you have, not what you lack.
- Increase is God's desire, but preparation is your responsibility.
- God is not withholding oil—He is waiting for vessels.

Before you move forward, remember this, You …

- are not empty.
- are not behind.
- are not disqualified.
- are not overlooked.
- have oil.
- have potential.
- have something in your house that God is ready to breathe on.

This book will help you discover it, cultivate it, stretch it, and prepare it for overflow.

My prayer is simple:

May your faith rise.
May your capacity expand.
And may you become a vessel God can fill—again and again and again.

Welcome to the journey where heaven meets earth.

Welcome to the place where faith meets capacity.

— Dr. Jean Héder Petit-Frère

THE WIDOW'S SECRET: FAITH IN CRISIS

"Now there cried a certain woman of the wives of the sons of the prophets unto Elisha, saying, 'Thy servant my husband is dead; and thou knowest that thy servant did fear the Lord.'" (2 Kings 4:1)

Crisis has a way of revealing what comfort conceals. The widow in 2 Kings 4 did not come to Elisha because she wanted more oil. Her husband's death, the impending kidnapping of her sons, and the overwhelming weight of loss, debt, and desperation forced her to seek help. What she carried within her was invisible, overlooked, and buried beneath the heaviness of her present season.

Yet Scripture does not introduce her as a weak woman. It introduces her as *"the wife of a prophet."* Her identity was tied not to her crisis but to a legacy of faith.

Occasionally the greatest faith is not displayed in the absence of tears but in the decision to run toward the prophetic voice when everything else is falling apart.

Faith is not always loud.

Occasionally it arrives with trembling hands.

At times it is soaked in grief.

Sometimes it survives only as a whisper.

But faith that still moves toward God—even with questions—is faith that God can multiply.

Her Cry Was the Beginning of Her Miracle

The text says, *"There cried a certain woman…"*
Her cry was not a casual request. It was anurgent appeal, a demand for intervention, a signal that something inside her refused to surrender.

There is a cry **God cannot ignore.** Heaven recognizes this cry as genuine. A cry that says, *"I cannot stay where I am."*

The widow's cry is the cry of every believer who has ever stood between loss and promise, between debt and deliverance, and between emptiness and expectation.

God is not threatened by your cry. He is drawn to it.

David said, *"This poor man cried, and the Lord heard him and saved him out of all his troubles."* (Psalm 34:6)

Your cry may be born /out of pain, but it carries the DNA of breakthrough.

When Crisis Meets Covenant
The widow appealed to Elisha based on covenant: *"Thy servant, my*

husband, feared the Lord."

She was not asking for charity. She was invoking spiritual legitimacy. She was reminding the prophet—and heaven—of the man her husband was.

When you have walked uprightly, heaven keeps record. When you have feared the Lord, your labor is never in vain. When you have served faithfully, God honors the seed even after the Sower is gone.

Her husband's devotion became her legal footing.

This is why Scripture declares, *"The memory of the righteous shall be blessed"* (Proverbs 10:7).

God does not forget your sacrifice, your service, or your fear of Him. Your obedience becomes generational currency.

Debt: The Silent Devourer of Destiny

The widow's crisis was not only emotional—it was financial. *"The creditor has come to take my two sons..."*

Debt is more than a financial issue. It is a destiny devourer. It steals future potential, attempts to enslave generations and poses a threat to disrupt inheritance at its core.

Her sons represented her future, lineage, household strength and place in society

Losing them meant losing everything. But God never allows the enemy to threaten your future without already having a plan to protect it.

Crisis Exposes What You Truly Have

Elisha's response is almost offensive: *"Tell me, what do you have in your house?"* (2 Kings 4:2)

To a grieving widow drowning in debt, this question felt insensitive. But Heaven always begins miracles with inventory, not sympathy.

God will not multiply what you hope for—He multiplies what you already have.

Your miracle is rarely somewhere else. It is often hiding in your own house. Your …

1. gift.
2. skill.
3. seed.
4. relationship.
5. idea.
6. potential.
7. oil.

The widow thought she had *"nothing… except a little jar of oil."* That "little" was Heaven's starting point.

Never underestimate the divine possibilities hidden inside something small.

Faith Always Begins With Honesty

The widow told the truth: *"I have nothing… except…"*

Miracles require truth-telling. God cannot bless who you pretend to be. Breakthrough begins where honesty begins.

For some, the "nothing except…" is:

- "I have nothing except the little strength I have left."
- "I have nothing except this small idea."
- "I have nothing except a broken marriage that still has love in it."
- "I have nothing except my willingness to try again."

Truth unlocks miracles.

The Widow's Secret

Her secret was not her oil. Her secret was her faith in crisis.

She chose to cry to the right source, speak truthfully, move despite fear, and trust a prophetic instruction she did not understand.

Faith does not remove crisis. Faith moves you through crisis.

The widow teaches us that when life collapses, faith must rise. Not loud, not dramatic, not polished, just willing. Because faith that is willing becomes faith that is multiplied.

Summary

This chapter examines the widow's period of despair, as well as the divine pattern concealed in misfortune. Her emptiness provided an opportunity for God to intervene. Faith begins when human strength ends. God questioned her, "What do you have in your home?" This passage demonstrates that miracles often begin with what we already have. The chapter establishes the tone: awareness, honesty, and surrender are the initial stages toward capacity.

Reflection Questions

1. What "crisis" in your life may actually be a doorway to expansion?
2. What do you already have in your "house" (skills, gifts, relationships) that you have overlooked?
3. In what areas have you allowed fear to silence your faith?
4. How can you shift from panic to prophetic perspective?
5. What small step of obedience can you take today to unlock your next level?

THE TWO QUESTIONS THAT CHANGE YOUR DESTINY

"Then he said, 'What shall I do for you? Tell me, what do you have in your house?'" (2 Kings 4:2)

Some moments in Scripture are so critical, so transformative, that the entire future of a person hinges on their response. In the widow's story, everything turns on two questions asked by the prophet Elisha—two questions that God is still asking every believer today.

These are not casual questions. They are *destiny* questions. They expose what is hidden beneath fear, grief, disappointment, and survival. They pull you into the realm where miracles begin.

Elisha did not pray first. He did not lay hands first. He did not prophecy first. He asked questions.

Why?

This is because God frequently employs questions to elicit revelation.

Jesus did the same. Jesus asked questions such as: *"Who do men say that I am?" "Do you believe I can do this?" "What do you want me to do for you? "Do you want to be made," whole?"*

Questions open doors that miracles walk through.

The First Question — "What Shall I Do for You?"

This question reveals two powerful realities:

1. God Honors Your Specificity

The prophet did not assume he knew what she needed. He did not say, "I know what you want," or "I see your situation." He asked, *"What do you want Me to do for you?"*

Heaven requires clarity. Faith must speak plainly.

General desires produce general results. Specific requests produce specific miracles.

Blind Bartimaeus cried, "Have mercy on me!" Jesus replied, "What do you want Me to do for you?" Not because He did not know but because your miracle is activated by your articulation.

The widow could have asked for comfort, protection, survival, justice or even money. But she asked for deliverance a breakthrough rooted in covenant and purpose.

2. God Invites You Into Partnership

Elisha did not ask this question because He was ignorant. He asked to draw the widow into participation.

God never moves in your life without inviting you into the process.

Your miracle involves your decision, faith, honesty, expectation, willingness to trust, and obedience.

The question "*What shall I do for you?*" is a divine invitation: "Tell me how you want me to intervene so I can align my power with your expectation."

The Second Question — "What Do You Have in Your House?"

This is the question that *separates dreamers* from achievers, spectators from participants, and the desperate from the delivered.

God does not begin with what you lack. He begins with what you have left.

The widow thought she had nothing of value. Her response was almost dismissive: *"I have nothing... except a small jar of oil."*

But God's economy is different. Little becomes much when placed in divine hands.

Miracles rarely begin externally. They begin internally; they begin with inventory.

Why These Two Questions Matter

Together, these questions uncover:

- What you want

- What you have
- What you believe
- What you are willing to offer
- Where your faith truly stands
- How God will move next

These are the two most important questions you will ever answer in a season of need.

1. **"What do you want?"** Reveals your focus.
2. **"What do you have?"** Reveals your capacity.

God aligns His miracles with desire and capacity. Wanting a miracle is not enough, you must locate your oil.

You Cannot Receive Until You Identify

The widow *had oil but could not see its value.*

The disciples had five loaves and two fish but *did not understand its potential.*

Moses had a *rod but did not realize its power.*

David had a *sling but did not recognize its anointing.*

God always asks,

3. "What is **in your hand**?"
4. "What **is in your house**?"

Because miracles flow through what you already possess.

What do you have? A gift, talent, connection, business idea, prayer life, voice, vision or a skill you stopped using.

You have something. Everyone does. Oil is never absent—only unnoticed.

The Questions That Change Your Destiny

Your answer to these questions determines the next chapter of your life.

1. What do you believe God can do for you today? Not someday. *Today.*
2. What do you have that God can use? Not what you lost. Not what others have. Not what you used to have. *What do you have NOW?*

These are the questions that transform crisis into capacity, lack into overflow, and despair into destiny.

Summary

This chapter highlights the two divine questions Elisha asked the widow: "What do you want?" And "What do you have?" Destiny turns on the clarity of desire and the honesty of inventory. God does not multiply confusion; He multiplies clarity. When you can articulate what you truly want and acknowledge what remains in your hand, you unlock Heaven's strategy. These two questions expose fear, refining vision, and activating capacity.

Reflection Questions

1. What do you truly want from God in this season—specifically?
2. Does your current lifestyle reflect what you say you desire?
3. What "little" do you have that God may want to use?
4. Where have you underestimated the value of what is already in your possession?
5. If God asked you these two questions today, how would you answer differently?

THE POWER OF A "BUT"

"...And she said, 'Thy handmaid hath not anything in the house, but a pot of oil.'" (2 Kings 4:2)

One of the smallest words in Scripture carries some of the greatest spiritual weight.

- It is a pivot word.
- It is a turning word.
- A destiny-shifting word.

That word is BUT.

In the widow's mouth, the "but" became the bridge between emptiness and possibility, between lack and abundance, and between despair and divine opportunity.

She said: *"I have NOTHING... **BUT** a small jar of oil."*

Most people stop at *"I have nothing."*

That is the language of defeat, discouragement, and resignation. But faith appears again. Faith digs deeper. Faith notices what others overlook.

Faith says: "*I may have nothing* but…" And everything after the "but" is what heaven uses.

"Nothing… BUT" — The Language of Miracles

In Scripture, whenever God is about to move, someone introduces a "but" that reframes the situation:

- "*We have nothing here… **BUT** five loaves and two fish.*"
- "*I cannot speak… **BUT** the Lord will be with my mouth.*"
- "*We have no wine… **BUT** there are six waterpots.*"
- "*There is no one else who can face him … **BUT** there is a boy with a sling.*"
- "*The army is too large… **BUT** send away the fearful.*"

Miracles begin when excuses end.

The "but" in your life reveals the seed God will multiply, the resource you dismissed, the gift you downplayed, the relationship you undervalued, the idea you abandoned, the strength you still have,

Your "but" is your doorway into divine strategy.

The "BUT" Reveals Your Leftover Capacity

The widow had lost her husband, stability, income, peace, security, reputation and hope.

She had a plan for the future. But she had oil—*small, insignificant, unnoticed, and unvalued.*

God never asks you for what you have lost. He asks for what remains. The "but" is where your remaining capacity hides.

It may not look like much, but:

- Every seed begins with something small.
- Every movement begins with one step.
- Every turnaround begins with one act of obedience.
- Every breakthrough begins with what you have left.

Your remaining capacity becomes heaven's material for your next miracle.

Faith Must Be Honest, But Faith Must Also Be expectant

The widow spoke truthfully:

- *"I have nothing…"* — her honesty
- *"…but a little oil."* — her expectation

Honesty brings accuracy. Expectation brings possibility.

Faith cannot grow in denial. But faith also cannot grow in defeat.

This is why your "but" matters. It holds both truth and hope in the same sentence.

For instance:

- "My marriage is struggling… BUT *we still love each other.*"
- "My finances are tight… BUT *God has always provided.*"
- "I feel weak… BUT *His strength is made perfect in weakness.*"
- "I feel overlooked… BUT *I still have a gift.*"

It is the pivotal point between human reality and divine potential.

Your "BUT" is a door that allows Heaven to enter

God always leaves you with **something to** use, surrender, activate, obey, pour, multiply.

The widow's "but" *revealed the one ingredient* God needed to release overflow.

Your miracle is never in what you *do not* have. It is in what you still have.

The Power of Recognizing Your "BUT"

The moment the widow said, *"…but a little oil,"* the direction of the entire story changed.

Her future was unlocked. Her prophetic instruction began.
Her sons' rescue was initiated.
Her capacity was identified.

Her miracle entered motion. Your "but" does the same. What is the "but" in your life? You may say …

- "I have little strength… but *I'm still standing.*"

- "I don't have much money… but *I have discipline.*"
- "I have no support… but I *have vision.*"
- "I am grieving… but I *still believe.*"
- "I am tired… but *I'm not quitting.*"

Whatever follows your "but" becomes the material for your next season.

The Widow's faith transformed at the moment of her "BUT"

She moved from crisis to possibility, despair to expectation, fear of participation,

She transitioned from a state of despair to one of expectation, and from fear to participation. All because she noticed what was left rather than what was lost.

Sometimes breakthrough does not come when your situation changes. The breakthrough comes when your perspective changes.

Your oil was never the problem. Your perspective was….

The Power of a "BUT" in Your Story

Every believer must eventually answer these questions:

- **What is left in** *my house?*
- **What is left in** *my hands*?
- **What is left in** *my spirit?*
- **What is left in** *my heart?*"

The moment you locate your "but "your miracle begins.

Summary

The woman informed him, "I am down to my last oil." After that "BUT" everything shifted.
From the depths of despair to your ultimate destiny, your "BUT" connects the two. God frequently uses the thing you least value to reveal a solution. Despite appearances to the contrary, this chapter demonstrates how the language of faith may transform our perspective on deficiency, restore faith, and unlock opportunities.

Reflection Questions

1. What negative confession in your life needs a faith filled "BUT"?
2. What small resource are you tempted to overlook?
3. How does your language shape your capacity?
4. Where is God asking you to stop focusing on what you lack?
5. What would shift if you reinterpreted your situation through faith rather than fear?

CHAPTER 4

THE OIL IN YOUR HOUSE

"And she said, 'Your servant has nothing in the house except a jar of oil.'" (2 Kings 4:2 (ESV)

There are moments in our lives when the noise of crisis becomes so loud that it blinds us to the resources God has already placed within our reach. The widow searched her entire house with the eyes of loss, not the eyes of faith. She saw only emptiness, only the absence of what once was.

But when God looked at her house, He saw oil. God saw *potential, capacity* - a *miracle* waiting for recognition.

Sometimes the greatest breakthroughs are not discovered, they are remembered. This is due to their constant presence.

The Oil Was Not New, It Was Neglected

The widow did not say, "*I don't have oil.*" She said, "*I have nothing* **except** *a little oil.*"

That small jar of oil represented what she had left, she had overlooked, she had undervalued, she still had access to, God intended to use.

Her miracle did not come from outside sources; it came from what was already inside her home.

- Just like Moses' rod.
- Just like David's sling.
- Just like Gideon and his three hundred men.
- Just like the loaves and fish.
- Just like the alabaster jar.
- Just like the small cloud Elijah saw, it was the size of a man's hand.

God always uses what remains.

The issue was not the oil itself; it was her perception of its value.

Oil Represents What God Has Already Given You

Oil in Scripture symbolizes:

- anointing,
- ability,
- giftings,
- calling,
- divine enablement,
- prophetic potential,
- spiritual inheritance.

The widow had oil, but she did not know its worth. Many believers live the same way, they have gifts but call them "nothing, strengths but minimize them, ideas but never act on them, dreams but bury them under discouragement, passions but dismiss them as irrelevant, and skills but underestimate their value.

Heaven begins miracles by revealing what you still have, NOT what you lost.

Your Oil May Look Small, But It Is Always Sufficient

The widow's oil was "little." But in God's economy, small is never a limitation—it is a doorway.

Jesus said: *"The kingdom of heaven is like a mustard seed…"*

A grain so tiny it can be blown away by wind, yet it contains the potential for forests.

Nothing has to be large for God to use it. It just has to be recognized and surrendered.

What Is the "Oil" in Your House?

Every believer has oil—something God can use: God can use a talent, skill, relationship, or prayer life?

Do you have a disciplined habit? A dream you have stopped believing in. A business idea buried under fear. A ministry call you have not activated.

A small open door you have not walked through yet?

Your miracle never begins with what is outside your house. It begins with the oil God placed inside you.

The question is not "Do I have oil?"

The question is: "Have I recognized my oil?"

You are *never as empty as you feel.* God ensures there is always a seed, a remnant, a starting point inside your "house." Always.

Why We Struggle to See Our Oil

The widow did not recognize the value of her oil because:

- Her emotions were *louder* than her faith.
- Grief and fear can *fog perception.*
- Her crisis overshadowed her *capacity.*
- Pain shrinks *awareness.*
- She compared her lack with *others' abundance.*
- Comparison kills recognition.
- She underestimated what *appeared small.*
- We often trust what looks big and ignore what looks *insignificant.*
- She concentrated on the problem rather than the *potential solutions.*
- She saw creditors; God saw *containers.*

Many believers do the same. Instead of asking, *"What do I have?"* They ask, *"Why don't I have more?"* The secret is simple: Miracles begin with what you have, not with what you lack. Your oil serves as a clue to your assignment.

- Oil in Scripture always aligns with *identity and purpose.*
- David was *anointed to lead.*
- Elisha was *anointed to prophesy.*
- The priests were *anointed to minister.*
- Kings were *anointed to govern.*
- Jesus was *anointed to preach the good news.*

Oil reveals who you are, what you are called to do, where your impact lies, what heaven expects from you.

Your oil is not random. It is PROPHETIC. It is intentional and divine. And it is already inside your house.

The Miracle Was Already in Motion

The *moment* the widow acknowledged her oil, the miracle began.

She has not yet borrow vessels. She had not yet shut the door. She did not yet pour. But the moment she recognized she had oil, the instruction came. Recognition always precedes revelation.

Some of the greatest breakthroughs in your life will begin when you stop saying: *"I have nothing."* and begins saying: *"I have oil."* God cannot use what you refuse to acknowledge.

The Oil In Your House Is Enough For The Next Season.

The widow went from: poverty to provision, despair to direction, loss to legacy.

She went from feeling emptied to *overflowing.* And all of it began with the oil she already had.

Your next season will not be built on, what people give to you, you wish you had, or what others possess.

Your miracle will be built upon the resources you possess. What God places in your house is always sufficient to initiate your miracle.

Summary

This chapter demonstrates how to achieve heavenly growth utilizing what you already have. The widow's oil represented character, gift, purpose, and the potential to do extraordinary things. Everything becomes more essential when you entrust your life to God. Your "oil" is often right in front of you, waiting to be discovered and used.

Reflection Questions

1. What gift or ability have you underestimated?
2. Who helped pour oil into your life, shaping who you are today?
3. What are the unique strengths God has placed inside your "house"?
4. What is one way you can begin to activate your oil this week?
5. How would your life change if you took your oil seriously?

DISCOVER YOUR OIL

"Tell me, what do you have in your house?" (2 Kings 4:2 (ESV)

Every miracle in the widow's life began with a single question: "What do you have in your house?"

God did not start with what she lacked, He started with *what she possessed.*

He did not begin with scarcity; He began *with seed.*

He did not focus on her pain; He focused on her *potential.*

This question is the hinge on which the entire story turns; it is the awakening moment. The moment where *revelation* meets responsibility, the moment where *despair* gives way to destiny!

Your oil is not something you must go find, your oil is something you must recognize.

It is already in your house, life, story, and hands.

Your oil is your divine advantage.

Discovering Your Oil Begins With Awareness

Most people overlook what God has already given them because, it looks too small, too ordinary, too familiar, too insignificant, or too common.

But the miraculous rarely begins with abundance, it begins with what seems small.

- Moses' rod
- David's sling
- Jacob's lunch
- Gideon's strength
- Paul's intellect
- A widow's oil

The smallness of your gift is not a sign of weakness, but a sign of divine intentionality.

God hides greatness in small beginnings.

Why People Fail to Recognize Their Oil

The widow said, *"I have nothing…"* Then immediately corrected herself: "…except a jar of oil."

Her oil was hidden beneath grief, trauma, fatigue, disappointment, fear, self-doubt.

Many believers *do not see their oil* because their pain speaks louder than their potential.

Pain blinds.
Grief distorts.
Fear diminishes.
Comparison suffocates.
Past failures deceive.

But your oil is stronger than your history. Your calling is *louder* than your *trauma*. Your potential is *greater* than your *pain*.

God sees what you overlook.

Your Oil Is Your God-Given Gift

Oil represents what God placed inside you to bless others and sustain your life: talents, skills, ideas, insight, spiritual gifts, wisdom, creativity, experience, grace, passion, calling, anointing, temperament, personality strengths and/or unique perspective.

Your oil is the divine deposit that makes you, YOU! It is the treasure hidden in your *earthly vessel*.

You are not empty, You are gifted.

You are not ordinary, You are anointed.

You are not random, You are intentional.

Signs of Your Oil

- Your oil is often found in what …
- comes easily to you but it is difficult for others.

- you do naturally without forcing it.
- others consistently seek you for (advice, help, clarity, support, and creativity).
- brings you deep joy? or righteous frustration.
- you feel spiritually responsible for.
- you can talk about, think about, or work for hours.
- God keeps highlighting through dreams, prophecy, or divine nudges.
- your story has prepared you for a struggle or breakthrough.
- produces results in others when you do it.

RECOGNITION is the first step toward multiplication.

Your Oil Is Connected to Your Assignment

- Your oil is not random; it is assignment specific.
- Joseph's oil was administration.
- Daniel's oil was wisdom.
- Esther's oil was influential.
- David's role was leadership.
- Solomon's oil was discernment.
- Deborah's oil was strategy and governance.
- Paul's oil was revelation and teaching.
- The widow's oil was entrepreneurial potential.

God gives you oil, which *aligns with the purpose* He designed you to fulfill. Your oil reveals your destiny.

Your Oil Is Often Found in Your History

Sometimes your oil is hidden in, your upbringing, habits, pain, survival skills, triumphs, mistakes, victories, encounters with God.

Your story is not accidental; it is usually *birthed from your experiences.*

Moses' oil of leadership came from both palace and wilderness. Joseph's oil of governance came from pits, prisons, and palaces. Your oil is a result of everything you have survived.

Nothing in your life is wasted. Oil is extracted from crushed olives. Your oil is *extracted from your crushed seasons.*

Questions That Help You Discover Your Oil

To awaken your oil, ask yourself, what ...

- **do I consistently do well with little effort?**
- **do people always thank me for it?**
- **problems do I solve naturally?**
- **have I developed through struggle or pain?**
- **skill or ability have I improved over time?**
- **makes me come alive spiritually?**
- **frustrates me when done poorly?**
- **would I still do even if I were not paid?**
- **do I feel "graced" to do?**
- **doors open naturally for me?**

Your oil becomes more visible the more *honest you are with these questions.*

Your Oil Has Economic Value

The widow's oil was not only spiritual—It became financial. Many believers separate their gift from the marketplace. But the first divine instruction regarding oil was: "Sell the oil."

Meaning – Your gift can sustain you, fund your family, underwrite your calling, become your business and break generational poverty.

Your oil carries value in ministry, marketplace, relationships, leadership, creativity, entrepreneurship, community, and impact!

Your oil is not just who you are—It is what God has given you to bring value to your world.

Your Oil Must Be Activated

Recognition without activation leads to stagnation.

You must do what the widow did:

- **Acknowledge your oil.**
- **Gather vessels (increase your capacity).**
- **Shut the door (protect your environment).**
- **Pour (use the gift).**
- **Fill every vessel (maximize opportunity).**
- **Sell the oil (move into assignment).**
- **Live on the rest (sustain the calling).**

Your oil is *not a museum piece*; it is a *tool of destiny*.

The world is *waiting* for the oil you carry.

Summary

This chapter guides the reader in identifying their unique gifting, passion, calling, and spiritual assignment. Everyone has oil, but many never recognize it. Through introspection, prayer, feedback, and observation, you discover the divine deposit that sets you apart. Your oil is your destiny clue.

Reflection Questions

1. What activities feel natural and life-giving to you?
2. What do others consistently affirm about your strengths?
3. What frustrates you deeply, often revealing your calling?
4. What opportunities keep showing up around you?
5. How is God highlighting your unique contribution to others?

BORROWING CAPACITY: SYSTEMS, STRUCTURES, AND MENTORS

"Then he said, 'Go outside, borrow vessels from all your neighbors, empty vessels—and not too few.' (2 Kings 4:3 (ESV)

Your oil determines your identity, but your capacity determines your outcome. Meaning:

- The widow had oil but *no vessels.*
- She had potential but had *no structure.*
- She had anointing but *no system* to contain it.
- She had a miracle in her house but had *no strategy to multiply it.*

The oil was enough for a miracle, but *not enough for the future* until vessels were added.

Elisha did not say, "Pray about more oil." He said, *"Borrow more capacity."*

Did you know?

- Miracles *require partnership.*
- Overflow *requires infrastructure.*
- Increase *requires collaboration.*

Why Borrowing Was Necessary

God could have filled the widow's house with new vessels. He could have sent angels to drop containers at her door. He could have produced barrels of oil supernaturally. But He did not. *Instead,* He instructed her to borrow.

Why? This is because God's purpose was to expand her capabilities, not to ensure her comfort.

Borrowing vessels teaches several Kingdom truths, you do not grow alone - Increase requires community. You do not rise without humility - Borrowing requires asking. You do not expand without relationships. - Your next season is tied to people. You do not multiply without systems. - Oil without vessels is waste. You do not reach destiny without mentors. - The prophet gave her direction; her neighbors gave her capacity.

Borrowing is not a sign of weakness. It is a sign of *wisdom.*

Capacity Is Never Built in Isolation

The widow was instructed to go to her neighbors - *Not angels. Not strangers.*

This rule also applies to other widows. Her neighbors. God enhances your life through the support of those closest to you. Even for those who may not understand your calling, anointing, journey or season.

You sometimes need vessels for your next level, and they are in the homes of people who do not know what God is about to do through you.

This is why the instruction matters: *"Borrow vessels…"*

This instruction is crucial—not just one, not just enough, but as many as possible.

Your miracle is *limited* only by your *capacity*.

Borrowing Capacity Means Borrowing Systems

Vessels are not just containers. They represent systems, processes, structure, organization, discipline, financial, order, emotional, capacity, relational, maturity, mentorship, and accountability.

Miracles are sustained by structure. Oil is held by vessels. Blessing is preserved by boundaries. Without vessels, oil becomes a mess. Without *structure,* increase becomes loss. Without *systems,* success becomes stress.

Many people are anointed, gifted, and called but not prepared.

Their oil is real, but their vessels are few.

Borrowing capacity is the ability to leverage systems and structures you did not create—systems you learn, taught by mentors, or adopt through exposure.

It means:

- learning from leaders,
- adopting new habits,
- receiving mentorship,
- applying wisdom,
- embracing accountability.

It means upgrading your inner infrastructure, to match your divine assignment.

Borrowing Requires Humility

The instruction to borrow did not honor the widow's pride—it crushed it. She had to knock on doors while her creditors were threatening her family. She had to say: "*Do you have an empty vessel I can borrow?*" "I need what you are not using." "I need your capacity."

Occasionally God will humble you before He elevates you.

This tendency is due to the fact that humility expands capacity more quickly than talent ever can.

Borrowing forces you to confront insecurity accept help lean on the community. Let others see your need. Keep your heart open to receive support and build bridges to receive wisdom

You cannot achieve abundance while remaining isolated.

The widow's miracle involved movement toward others.

Your next level will involve the same.

Your Next Level Depends on Who You Borrow From

Not all neighbors carry the vessels you need. Borrowing is prophetic, strategic, and destiny-shaping.

You must borrow:

- Wisdom from mentors
- Discipline from leaders
- Insight from spiritual fathers
- Excellence from those who walk in it
- Faith from those who have proven God.
- Order from those who are structured
- Vision from those who see further.

Growth requires association. Elevation requires proximity. Increase requires connection.

The widow borrowed vessels from her neighbors. However, her instructions were given by her prophet.

You need *neighbors for capacity*. but mentors for direction.

Why is "Not a Few" important?

This phrase is loaded with prophetic weight. Elisha insisted: *"Borrow vessels—not **a few**."*

Why? Because God was about to pour according to her preparation, not according to her desperation.

Heaven responds to faith expressed as capacity, *not emotion*.

Her preparation determined her *overflow*. Her capacity determined the *quantity*. Her obedience determined the *outcome*.

The widow's miracle had no divine limit—The only limit was the number of vessels she gathered.

This verse is still true today: God will fill everything you prepare. No more. No less.

Borrowing Capacity Today

What does it mean for you? Borrowing capacity may look like:

- learn financial discipline.
- partner with someone stronger in the organization.
- sitting under mentorship.
- take a course.
- join a team.
- seeking counsel
- reorganizing your life
- healing emotionally
- reading what you have never read
- adopting new strategies
- change your environment.
- raise your standards.

Asking for help does not weaken you. It expands you.

Borrowing is not a sign of deficiency—It is the starting point of destiny.

Borrowing Capacity Creates Generational Change

The widow did not solely create the debt that threatened her home— she inherited it.
Her husband probably died under the weight of obligations he could no longer carry, and now the collectors came for her sons, the last remaining pieces of her future.

But though she inherited financial debt, she chose to borrow capacity—vessels, instructions, wisdom, and divine strategy.

She borrowed not money, but a new way of thinking, a new level of obedience, a new system for increase, a new pathway for generational preservation.

Her borrowed vessels became the bridge between her *crisis* and her *future*.

Your willingness to borrow capacity— to learn what you were never taught, to embrace wisdom you did not grow up with, to adopt systems you never inherited— will rescue your children from the limitations you once lived under.

Just as her borrowed vessels secured her sons' future, the wisdom you borrow today becomes the inheritance your children will live with from tomorrow.

Summary

The widow had oil but lacked vessels. God's instruction forced her into community, humility, and partnership. This chapter shows that no destiny is fulfilled alone. Capacity grows through mentors, systems, and people who carry what you need. Increase flows in networks, not isolation.

Reflection Questions

1. Who are the people whose vessels you need to borrow?
2. Where is God calling you to ask for help or seek mentorship?
3. Which relationships no longer support your next level?
4. What systems or structures do you need to build or borrow?
5. How has pride or fear held you back from collaboration?

BORROWING VESSELS WELL

"Then he said, 'Go outside, borrow vessels from all your neighbors, empty vessels—and not too few.'" (2 Kings 4:3 (ESV)

Borrowing vessels was not a random action - It was a divine strategy.

It required humility, relationship, wisdom, discernment, and obedience.

It required emotional strength and social intelligence. It required the ability to *partner with people* for a miracle they would not witness and a breakthrough they would not experience directly.

Borrowing vessels was not merely a *physical task,* it was a relational test. A test of humility, credibility, trust, stewardship, community, vision, maturity.

The miracle required oil, but the oil required vessels, and the vessels required people. The widow needed God, but she also needed neighbors. Increase requires heaven but it also requires community.

Borrowing Is an Act of Humility

Borrowing is *uncomfortable,* it exposes need, it *requires asking,* it *demands vulnerability.*

A proud person cannot borrow well.

The widow had to *knock on doors,* while her *reputation* was shaken and her circumstances were humbling.

She was financially broken, emotionally drained, spiritually wounded and socially embarrassed.

Yet *she asked anyway.*

Humility *enlarges capacity, while* pride limits miracles.

God often hides increase, behind the humility of asking for help.

Borrowing Requires Discernment

Not every neighbor carried the right vessel. Some vessels were unusable, however the relationships between neighbors were healthy. The door was strategic.

Borrowing vessels *well demands discernment:*

The widow should be asking the "Who" questions. Who has the capacity you need? Who carries wisdom you must learn? Who holds insight you lack? Who can mentor you? Who stretches your vision? Who expands your thinking? Who strengthens your character? Who pushes you toward purpose?

Some vessels come from neighbors you love, others come from neighbors you least expect.

Discernment is not suspicion— It is *alignment*.

God will send the right people, when your *heart is ready for increase.*

Borrowing Well Means Borrowing Widely

Elisha said, "Borrow vessels… and not too few."

Meaning – Do not borrow small, narrowly, limited, afraid, hesitantly, reluctantly, or with a survival mindset.

Borrow like someone EXPECTING A MIRACLE.

Borrowing vessels required boldness. It required expanding her relational circle, knocking on doors she had never knocked on before and involving neighbors who may not have liked her.

To borrow well is to increase your relational capacity.

Many believers stay small because they only connect with people who look like them, think like them, affirm them, or comfort them. But the miracle required expansion.

She could not limit her destiny to familiar environments.

Borrowing Requires Emotional Maturity
Borrowing vessels required the widow to handle rejection, questions, judgement, curiosity, criticism and awkwardness.

Some neighbors ***probably asked:***

"Why do you need this?"
"What will you do with it?"
"Can you return it?"
"Are you sure you can handle it?"

Emotional maturity is the ability to see beyond the moment and focus on the miracle.

Borrowing requires maturity to stay focused, calm, grateful, patient, and determined. The immature mind avoids discomfort; the *mature mind* embraces the process.

Borrowing Vessels Is Borrowing Capacity

Every vessel represented something she lacked: time, experience, preparation, wisdom, structure, systems, insight, understanding, help, or support

When you *borrow vessels,* you borrow what *others cultivated.*

You borrow the strength of *someone else's discipline.*

You borrow the wisdom of someone *else's history.*

You borrow the structure, of someone *else's preparation.*

You borrow capacity, until you *develop your own.*

Borrowing is not dependency—It is development.

EXAMPLES:

A young minister without administrative skill may borrow structure

from a seasoned leader until he grows into his own capacity.

A new entrepreneur may borrow business models, until she builds her own.

A family may borrow principles from mentors, until those principles become internal identity.

The widow's borrowed vessels were temporarily scaffolding for her permanent miracle.

Borrowing Well Means Returning What You Borrowed

Integrity is the *hidden key*, behind every sustainable miracle.

The text implies something powerful: - If she borrowed the vessels, she would eventually return them.

This means, she honored relationships, valued trust, respected her neighbors, protected her reputation, maintained divine order and preserved relational capital.

The kingdom expands through *relational integrity*.

A miracle that damages relationships is not a 'Kingdom miracle.'

Returning what you borrow, shows character.

Living honorably after increasing shows maturity.

Borrowing Vessels Well in Your Own Life

To borrow vessels well on your journey, you must Identify who carries what you lack: Nobody grows alone. Ask with humility: It takes strength to request help. Observe with discernment: Not every vessel fits your destiny. Expand beyond your comfort zone: Growth requires courage. Build relational credibility: People trust what you consistently model. Protect relationships through integrity: Never burn a bridge God may use again. Stay grateful for every borrowed vessel. Honor opens future doors.

Borrowing vessels well is **not a sign of weakness**—It is the *sign of someone preparing for greatness.*

Summary

Borrowing requires humility, discernment, and relational wisdom. This chapter explores how to borrow the right vessels—mentors, systems, models, partnerships, and resources—without losing integrity or identity. The goal is to grow through others while remaining authentic to your own oil.

Reflection Questions

1. Who are the mentors or leaders you should seek out right now?
2. What systems or ideas could you borrow to increase your capacity?
3. Which relationships elevate you—and which drain you?
4. How can you honor those who lend you their "vessels"?
5. What fears keep you from asking for help?

SHUTTING THE DOOR: PRIVATE OBEDIENCE

"Then go in, shut the door behind yourself and your sons, and pour into all these vessels." (2 Kings 4:4 (ESV)

There are miracles that God performs in public, and there are miracles that God conceals behind closed doors.

There are blessings God displays before your enemies. And there are breakthroughs God develops in secrecy.

Some of the most profound transformations of your life will happen where no one can see you, no applause, validation, audience or a crowd.

It was just you, your oil, your sons, and your God.

The instruction to "shut the door" was not a suggestion. It was a requirement. Because there are dimensions of glory, depth, deliverance, and multiplication that only flow in the privacy of obedience.

Why the Door Had to Be Shut

Elisha understood something the widow did not see: Some environments can suffocate miracles. There were several reasons she had to close the door:

1. To Protect the Miracle From Doubters.
    Neighbors could lend her vessels. but they could not handle her process. Every believer must learn this: Some people can support your capacity but cannot witness your transformation.
    Doubt is *contagious*. Fear is *transferable*. Skepticism can *poison* a miracle before it begins.
    God desired her oil to flow in an environment free from judgment, comparison, unbelief, commentary, opinions, and interference.
    Some people may love you but not be safe for your wonder because they do not share your vision, they may doubt or be negative about you, they may judge or compare your path to others', or they may obstruct your growth. Their limited viewpoint, which stems from their personal issues or experiences, may keep you from reaching your full potential for miracles.
    The door you close behind you is just as important as the oil you pour before you. Protect your miracle from voices not assigned to your destiny.

2. To Teach Her Sons the Value of Obedience
   Her sons were about to carry on with the family's legacy. They needed to see her faith, feel her obedience, witness her sacrifice, and experience the oil firsthand.
   Behind closed doors, children learn integrity, humility, faith, discipline, prayer, honor and resilience.
   Some of the greatest impartations in your life will come behind closed doors where only your spiritual sons and daughters can see your obedience.

3. To Create an Environment for Raw faith.
   Public faith is easy to express, but private faith comes with a price, as it requires deep *personal conviction and sacrifices* that go beyond mere outward appearances.
   Behind closed doors, your tears can fall freely, doubts have been confronted, fears are exposed, worship becomes real, and prayers become honest.
   Walls do not limit miracles, they *shield* them.
   For many believers, God is trying to increase their oil, but their *door is too wide open.*
   There are simply too many distractions and too many voices. The abundance of opinions is overwhelming. The number of interruptions is excessive. Despite her steadfast faith and attempts to remain composed, there are several occasions of emotional leakage.
   A shut door is a sacred space. A place of consecration,

focus, and surrender.

Miracles often begin with confidentiality

Jesus often shut the door before performing miracles. He …

- put unbelievers out before raising Jairus' daughter.
- took the blind man away from the crowd before healing him.
- prayed alone on the mountain before walking on water.
- poured out His soul in Gethsemane away from the multitude.

The principle is consistent: Some miracles require privacy for *clarity*.

The widow's oil was *not meant to flow* where fear or skepticism could interfere.

God sealed her in a faith environment, a prophetic womb so the oil could mature unhindered.

Behind Closed Doors, You Learn To Nurture

The miracle of multiplication did not happen in the marketplace. It happened behind a locked door.

Some believers say, "Lord, *use me publicly*." But God answers, *Obey Me privately*."

It is in secrecy that you learn to pour without applause, without validation, without fear, without comparison, and with only purity.

When you can pour privately, God can trust you publicly.

The widow's private obedience became her public testimony.

Shutting the Door Separates You From Your Past

When the widow closed the door, she shuts out, the fear of losing her sons, voices of anxiety, history of debt, weight of widowhood, sound of her own grieving, and pressure of her creditors.

A shut door is prophetic—*it signifies transition.*

- Behind the door: She was a grieving widow.
- When the door opened: She was an entrepreneur with a miracle supply chain.

The closed door does not signify the end of your journey; It is your metamorphosis.

Shutting the Door Forces You to Trust God Alone

There is no prophet in the room. There is no one nearby to lend a hand. There was no congregation present to offer prayers. There is no elderly people present to perform the anointing ceremony. There is only a widow, her children, and God.

This is the place where faith matures.

When all you have is God, you discover that God is *enough*.

Behind closed doors, He becomes your instructor, comforter, counselor and multiplier.

The door shuts on human support. so it can be opened to divine supply.

The Door Only Opens When the Miracle Is Finished

The Scripture says: *"She went in and shut the door behind herself and her sons … and as she poured, they brought the vessels to her." (2 Kings 4-5)*

The door remained shut, until the oil had finished flowing.

No one could interrupt, influence, or contaminate the environment.

Some processes in your life must remain hidden until God finishes His work.

Others cannot understand it until the oil stops, dust settles, and a miracle is complete. Instructions are fulfilled and season has shifted.

Some doors stay shut, because the miracle is still in process.

Summary

Elisha told the widow to *"shut the door"* behind her. Privacy protects miracles. Some instructions cannot survive public opinion, noise, or distraction. This chapter teaches the importance of protecting your process, guarding your atmosphere, and obeying God even when no one sees.

Reflection Questions

1. What door(s) do you need to shut to protect your next season?
2. Who or what introduces doubt into your obedience?
3. What private habits fuel your spiritual strength?
4. How does your atmosphere support or hinder God's flow?

5. What would change if you obeyed God more in private than in public?

POUR UNTIL IT STOPS: THE LAW OF DIVINE MULTIPLICATION

> *"So she went from him and shut the door behind herself and her sons. And as she poured, they brought the vessels to her. When the vessels were full, she said to her son, 'Bring me another vessel.' And he said to her, 'There is not another.' Then the oil stopped flowing.*
> (2 Kings 4:5–6 (ESV)

The most astonishing part of this miracle is not that the oil multiplied. The astonishing part is when it multiplied.

The oil did not multiply when the prophet spoke, when the vessels were gathered, when the door was shut, or when the room was prepared.

The miracle began when she poured.

The supernatural waited for her obedience. Heaven waited for her movement. God waited for her action.

Oil *responds to pouring.*

The Miracle Was Activated by Her hands

God *provided the oil.* God *ordained the vessels.* God *gave the instruction.* But God did not pour for her. Some *miracles* require your participation. Some *breakthroughs* require your movement. Some *seasons* will not begin until you start the action God commanded.

Many believers expect multiplication before they pour. But Scripture reveals the opposite:

- Abraham moved before he saw the ram.
- Peter cast his net before the fish appeared.
- Joshua stepped into the Jordan before the waters parted.
- The servants filled the jars before the water became wine.
- The widow poured before the oil increased.

Multiplication is always on the other side of obedient action.

Pouring Requires Faith
The widow stood over empty vessels with only a *tiny jar of oil.* Naturally, the math did not make sense. Spiritually, the miracle demanded it.

She had to believe that God would meet her motion, the supply would respond to the demand, the oil would honor the instruction and that God would fill what she dared to provide.

Pouring is an act of expectation, an act of courage and an act of partnership with Heaven.

When you pour, you are declaring God will meet me in this." And

He always does.

You Pour—God Multiplies!

The widow did what she could. God did what she could not.

This is the divine formula: You provide the action. God provides the multiplication.

You pour a little. God *produces the overflow.* This is why Scripture says: *"Faith without works is dead." (James 2:17)*

The oil would not have moved, until she moved.

The increase would not have begun, until she poured.

Some believers are waiting for God to move, but in truth, God is waiting for you to **pour** your gift, your service, out your excellence, out your obedience, your dedication, your vision. your time, and your worship.

Heaven multiplies only what you are willing to release.

As Long as There Was a Vessel—There Was Oil

This is a breathtaking truth. The oil did not stop because the oil ran out. The oil stopped, because the vessels ran out.

This means the miracle was not governed by heaven—It was governed by her capacity. The supply was unlimited; however the vessels were not. Heaven was ready to pour as long as she was ready to provide. This is one of the great mysteries of the Kingdom:

God fills everything you prepare, but He will not fill what you **refuse to present.**

The Oil Will Flow As Long As You Pour It

Your *ministry will flow, as long as you keep pouring. Your business will grow, as long as you keep pouring. Your anointing will increase, as long as you keep pouring. Your calling will expand, as long as you keep pouring. Your breakthrough will continue, as long as you keep pouring.*

The moment you stop pouring, you become passive, discouraged, or stagnant, and the oil stops. Not because God changed, but because motion stopped. Pouring is not an event; it is a *lifestyle.*

Pouring Requires Trust Beyond understanding

Nothing in the widow's situation made sense: - empty vessels, A little oil, A shut door, A clear instruction and a desperate need. But obedience does not require understanding, Only trust.

You cannot move into your next dimension while analyzing every detail. Some instructions only produce results when executed without hesitation.

Pouring is prophetic, trusting and surrendering your human logic to divine wisdom.

The Oil Stopped—But the Blessing Continued

When the last vessel was filled, the oil stopped, but her miracle did not. The multiplication ended but her provision began.

The *flow ended*, but her future started. The oil stopped but her debt was canceled. Her sons were saved and her life was transformed.

Some seasons in your life will *stop flowing* because the purpose of that particular season has been fulfilled. But the blessing remains: seasons end, miracles mature, purposes shift, and assignments evolve.

The oil stopping is not a loss. It is a transition.

Pour Until It Stops

- This is the command of every believer: Pour …
- your gift until the vessel is filled.
- out your obedience until the season shifts.
- out your excellence until the door opens.
- your worship until the atmosphere changes.
- your calling until the oil stops on its own.
- your faith until God says, "Enough—now watch Me."

Because pouring is not about supply, it is about surrender. Pour until God finishes what He started.

Summary

The miracle unfolded as she poured. Movement activated multiplication. God multiplies obedience, not hesitation, action, not intention. This chapter shows how faith becomes fruitful only through consistent, courageous pouring—into people, purpose, prayer, and preparation—until Heaven signals completion.

Reflection Questions

1. What area of your life needs consistent "pouring" right now?

2. Where have you stopped pouring too soon?
3. What fear has slowed your obedience?
4. How does movement increase your faith?
5. What would change if you poured until God, not circumstances, said "stop"?

KINGDOM ECONOMICS: SELL THE OIL

"Go, sell the oil and pay your debts, and you and your sons can live on the rest." (2 Kings 4:7 (ESV)

Every miracle in Scripture has a purpose beyond the moment. God never multiplies just for survival. He multiplies for *sustainability, stability, and future impact.*

The widow's miracle did not end with the pouring of oil. The miracle reached its full expression when God gave her something even more valuable:

A Divine Economic Strategy

Elisha did not simply say, "Rejoice in the miracle." He said, "Go, sell the oil."

This is the first recorded instance in Scripture where supernatural provision is immediately connected to entrepreneurship and financial management.

Her miracle was not just oil. Her miracle was a business plan.

God multiplied her oil but Elisha multiplied her wisdom.

Kingdom Economics Begins With "Go"

Elisha's instruction starts with movement:

"Go."

Before she could sell, before she could pay debt, before she could live freely— She had to move.

Miracles stagnate when the recipient refuses to act.

What God provides will often require: steps, decisions, planning, diligence, strategy, and work.

Faith is not passive; Faith *moves.*

Just as the oil did not multiply until she poured, her provision would not manifest until she went.

Many believers celebrate the oil but *never step into the marketplace* where the oil must be sold.

Supernatural breakthroughs become tangible provisions when obedience meets movement.

"Sell the" Oil"—The Divine Intersection of Faith and Business

God told the widow to do more than praise Him for the oil, He told her to monetize it.

This breaks a misconception many believers live with:

Spiritual anointing and economic productivity are not enemies. They are partners.

The God who multiplies your oil also instructs *you to turn it into income.*

The widow had a product, a supply, a market, an instruction, and a demand.

The oil was not for display. It was not for nostalgia. It was not for hoarding. It was for COMMERCE.

"Sell the oil" means, turn your gift into fruit, anointing into impact, capacity into profit, miracle into a system. Her jar became her *business*. Her miracle became her *provision*. Her obedience became her *prosperity*.

Elisha's next instruction is not emotional; it is economic warfare.

"Pay your debt." Debt is more than numbers – it is a spiritual weight, mental prison, a generational thief.

The widow's debt threatened not only her peace but her lineage.

The enemy always attempts to capture the next generation through financial bondage.

By paying her debt, she broke a generational curse, protected her children, closed the door to the enemy, restored dignity to her house, and stepped into freedom.

Your miracle is not complete until your finances are aligned with Kingdom order.

Deliverance is not only spiritual. Sometimes deliverance is *financial.*

"Live on the" Rest"—Sustainability, Not Survival

This is the part of the story *most believers overlook.*

Elisha said, "…and you and your sons can live on the rest." Not survive. Not struggling. Not scrape by but LIVE!

The miracle was designed to provide stability, restore dignity, secure the future, sustain her household and to give her sons a foundation.

This is Kingdom economics:

God does not bless you for one day. He blesses you for a lifetime.

The widow did not receive a one-time miracle, temporary fix, or a shallow breakthrough.

She received a strategy that positioned her for long-term prosperity.

Her miracle was not emotional, it was structural.

Structure established a **lifestyle, business, future, and legacy.**

God's goal is not just your breakthrough. His goal is your built-up life.

Miracles Require Management

The pouring of oil was supernatural, selling the oil was practical, paying the debt was responsible and living on the rest was strategic.

This is the partnership of heaven and earth:

God *pours* - You steward.

God *multiplies* - You manage.

God *opens doors* - You walk through them.

God *provides oil* - You develop systems.

God *releases miracles* - You build structure around them.

A *miracle without stewardship* is a wasted opportunity. A miracle with management becomes a generational blessing.

Kingdom Economics in Your Life Today

"Sell the oil" may look like launching your business, using your gift professionally, stepping into entrepreneurship, creating structure around your calling, monetizing your skill, being excellent in the marketplace, breaking out of poverty mindsets, paying off your debts, and securing your children's future.

God is not glorified by your struggle. He is glorified by your stewardship.

The widow's economic breakthrough began when she obeyed the prophetic instruction to turn her miracle into movement. Yours will begin the same way.

Summary

The prophet told her not just to pour but to sell. God is strategic: spiritual miracles unlock practical solutions. This chapter teaches that the Kingdom honors stewardship, enterprise, value exchange, and responsible prosperity. Increase is meant to be managed, not merely celebrated.

Reflection Questions

1. What skills or gifts could be monetized or stewarded better?
2. How does your mindset manage prosperity, fear or faithfulness?
3. Are you managing your resources with Kingdom wisdom?
4. What systems do you need to build to "sell the oil"?
5. How does financial stewardship reflect spiritual maturity?

THE LIMIT OF OIL IS THE LIMIT OF VESSELS

"When the vessels were all full, she said to her son, 'Bring me another vessel.' But he answered, 'There is not another.' Then the oil stopped." (2 Kings 4:6 (ESV)

Every miracle in the Kingdom carries a divine rhythm. Heaven pours according to the space you create. God fills according to the preparation you make. The supernatural responds to the capacity you bring.

The widow's story is a masterclass in kingdom dynamics: The oil did not run out. The vessels did.

The limitation was not divine, it was human.

The restriction was not heaven's unwillingness; It was her available capacity.

If she had gathered more vessels, more oil would have flowed.

This is one of the most sobering truths in Scripture:

Your supply is determined by your capacity, not by God's power.

God Never Stopped Pouring—She Stopped Presenting

The miracle did not end because God closed the faucet. It ended because she ran out of containers.

Imagine the tension of that moment:

The oil was still ready to flow…but it had nowhere to go.

Many **believers experience this divine tension today; you feel** the anointing but lack structure, sense the calling but lack discipline, carry ideas but lack planning, have vision but lack systems, and want expansion but resist preparation.

The oil is not the problem. CAPACITY is.

The Kingdom does not reward desire—It rewards preparation.

Your Capacity Sets the Boundaries of Your Life

This truth applies to every realm:

1. **Spiritual Capacity**
   God pours revelation according to your hunger. Your depth in the Spirit matches your depth in devotion, discipline, and consecration.

2. **Emotional Capacity**
   Some people cannot maintain relationships not because they lack love but because they lack emotional containers.

3. **Financial Capacity**

   God cannot bless what you *cannot* manage.

   Income follows structure.

   Provision follows stewardship.

4. **Leadership Capacity**

   Your ability to lead others is tied to your ability to lead yourself.

5. **Vision Capacity**

   Some see only vessels. Others see *opportunities*. Your vision determines your *vessel count*.

Throughout Scripture, God always multiplies based on capacity:

- Israel received land based on their numbers.
- The talents increased based on management.
- The people were fed based on organization (in groups of fifties and hundreds).
- The early church grew based on the apostles' ability to structure.

Your destiny is *not limited by opposition*— It is limited by the size of your containers.

The Oil Will Always Reveal Your Real Capacity

Many people *think they are ready for more*, but the oil will tell the truth.

Oil exposes, the gaps in your preparation, cracks in your systems, weakness in your foundation, limits in your mindset, borders of your discipline, or the size of your commitment.

If you want more oil, increase your capacity.

You do not pray for oil. You prepare for oil.

God sends oil to the level of your vessels.

The Miracle Responded to Preparation, Not Emotion

Nothing in the story suggests that God multiplied the oil because the widow was desperate or emotional.

She cried out but the miracle responded to her obedience, not her tears.

Desperation moved her to seek the prophet. But preparation moved the oil.

God responds to faith expressed in action.

Heaven respects order fills what is empty and pours into what is ready.

Emotion may touch God's heart but preparation attracts His power.

Capacity Is a Partnership Between You and God

The prophet did not say: "Sit and watch God fill whatever He wants." He said: *"Gather vessels."*

The implication is clear: God decides the oil. You decide on the vessels.

The widow did not need to produce oil. She needed to produce space.

This is Kingdom partnership.

God gives the supernatural supply and you *build the natural structure.* God sends growth and you *create order.* God opens doors and you *walk through them.* God blesses and *you manage.*

Running Out Of Vessels Does Not Signify Failure; Rather, It Reveals Deeper Truths

When she reached the last vessel, it did not mean she failed. It meant she discovered the limit of her previous season.

Every believer will reach a moment where you realize, "I need more discipline," "I need more skill," "I need better structure," "I need stronger accountability," "I need deeper mentorship, "and "I need greater planning."

This revelation is *not condemnation* but an invitation. A new season always *demands new vessels.*

Capacity Must Always Grow With Assignment

You cannot face new levels with old containers, walk into new opportunities with old systems, or handle new blessings with old habits.

Every assignment God brings requires new vessels, preparation, thinking, structure, discipline, and responsibility. The oil is unlimited but your *season requires* you to enlarge your capacity.

This is why Scripture repeatedly commands:

"Enlarge the place of your tent." (Isaiah 54:2)

"*Stretch out.*" "*Spare not.*"
"*Lengthen.*"
"*Strengthen.*"

Your *expansion is tied to your containers.*

Where Capacity Ends, Destiny Pauses

Not stops. Not dies. But pauses …The oil did not vanish; It simply waited for more vessels.

Some believers misinterpret silence as punishment when in reality it is an invitation.

God is not withholding more oil; He is waiting for more capacity. Increase your vessels, and your destiny will move again.

Summary

The flow of oil stopped only when the vessels ran out. God did not impose the limit—capacity did. This chapter addresses internal ceilings, structural limitations, small thinking, fear, and lack of preparation. God will not fill what you refuse to build.

Reflection Questions

1. What vessel (structure, system, habit) do you need to create next?
2. Where have you unintentionally limited God?
3. Which internal beliefs are shrinking your capacity?
4. What small daily changes could expand your vessels?
5. If God sent more oil today, would you be ready?

FAITH FOR HEAVEN, CAPACITY FOR EARTH

"Your kingdom come, Your will be done, on earth as it is in heaven."
(Matthew 6:10 (ESV))

Every believer stands between two realms:

1. Heaven's unlimited power
2. Earth's limited containers.

Faith connects you to Heaven. Capacity determines what reaches Earth.

God is *never short* of miracles, wisdom, resources, or a breakthrough.

But the Earth has limits in thinking, in planning, in discipline, in structure, in vision.

To walk in kingdom fullness you must master this divine equation: Faith is your access. Capacity is your ability. Faith *opens the heavens*. Capacity *receives what faith has accessed*.

Without *faith*, nothing is possible. Without *capacity*, nothing is sustainable.

Heaven Is Ready—Earth Must Make Room

When Jesus taught the disciples to pray, "Your will be done on earth as it is in heaven."
He was not giving them a religious confession—He was giving them adivine responsibility.

Heaven is always ready - Earth is not always prepared.

Heaven has alignment - Earth has disorder.

Heaven has clarity. - Earth has confusion.

Heaven has abundance. -Earth has scarcity.

Heaven has answers. - Earth has unreadiness.

Your calling as a Kingdom ambassador is to bring Earth to a place where it can receive what Heaven wants to release.

This requires more than prayer. It requires preparation.

Faith Gives You Permission—Capacity Gives You Possession

There is a major difference between *having the right to something and having the ability to receive it.*

Faith gives you the right. Capacity gives you the ability.

The widow's mind had to shift before her miracle could manifest.

A Poverty Mindset Ignores What God Has Already Given

Many believers pray for more while ignoring what they already have.

They ask God for miracles while *despising the little that is in their house.*

They *want the overflow* but *disregard the seed.*

A poverty mindset - magnifies lack, minimizes opportunity, focuses on what is missing, ignores what is present. It creates blindness to possibility. This is why the prophet first asked: "What do you have in your house?"

Your miracle begins with recognition.

God's multiplication requires your cooperation.

Your transformation begins when you see what God sees.

A Poverty Mindset Expects Loss More Than Possibility

The widow anticipated the worst and many believers live the same way.

Generational poverty trains the mind to fear the future, expect scarcity, assume failure, anticipate limitations, normalize struggle, glorify survival instead of growth.

Such a mind cannot perceive increases even when the increase sits

Faith says: "This promise is mine." "This miracle is available." "This breakthrough is possible."

Capacity asks:

"Do I have the structure to hold it?"
"Do I have the discipline to sustain it?"
"Do I have the systems to manage it?"
"Do I have the character to carry it?"

Faith reaches up. Capacity holds what faith brings down.

This is why so many people receive glimpses of what God wants to do—prophetic promises, dreams, revelations, visions and yet they cannot walk in the fullness of it.

They have faith, but not enough capacity.

God Does Not Send What You Cannot Sustain

Throughout Scripture, God *refuses* to pour into unprepared vessels: He did not ...

- send rain to Noah until the ark was built.
- send Israel into the Promised Land until Joshua organized tribes.
- pour out the Spirit until the disciples gathered in one accord.
- increase the early church until deacons were appointed.
- multiply the widow's oil until she gathered vessels.

Heaven waits for structure.

God is not withholding the miracle; He is *waiting for the vessel*.

The limitation is not in heaven—It is in us.

Faith for Heaven Without Capacity for Earth Creates Frustration

Many believers live with prophetic frustration:

They *sense* something great but cannot *walk* in it.

They feel called but cannot manifest.

They have vision, but no strategy.

They see the promise. but *cannot enter the land.*

Why? Because faith alone is not enough. Faith *opens the door*, but capacity walks through it.

Prophetic frustration is evidence that your spirit has seen the future that your mind and habits are not yet prepared to sustain. The solution is not more prophecy—but more capacity.

Capacity Is the Proof That You Expect God to Move

Anyone can say they believe, but capacity shows that you expect something waiting to happen.

The woman with the issue of blood believed, but she *pressed through the crowd.*

Blind Bartimaeus believed but he *cried out louder.*

Peter believed but he *stepped out of the boat.*

The widow believed but she *borrowed vessels.*

Faith without capacity is like faith without proof.

Faith Brings the Supernatural—Capacity Makes It Natural

Heaven is *not meant* to stay in heaven. It is meant to manifest through people and being equipped and prepared to handle it.

Faith connects you to the unseen. Capacity brings the unseen into the visible.

This is why God trains His people:

- Moses spent 40 years in Midian.
- David spent years with sheep.
- Joseph learned management in Egypt.
- Esther was prepared for 12 months.
- Paul was trained for years before ministry.
- Jesus grew in wisdom and stature before revealing His identity.

Heaven invests in preparation.

Faith accesses grace. Capacity manifests glory.

When Faith and Capacity Unite—The Earth Reflects Heaven

When these two forces meet, nothing in your life remains the same.

Faith without capacity is potential without outlet. Capacity without faith is effort without power. But faith and capacity together create breakthroughs, purpose fulfillment, generational transformation, divine partnership, and unstoppable momentum.

This is the mystery of Kingdom dominion:

Heaven opens by faith. Earth holds by capacity.

The widow's miracle demonstrates it perfectly:

- Faith brought her to the prophet.
- Capacity sent her to borrow vessels.
- Faith believed the oil would flow.
- Capacity made room for the oil to fill.

Your life must carry both. if you will walk in the fullness of what God intends.

Summary

Faith connects you to Heaven; capacity determines what reaches Earth. Heaven provides the oil; earth provides the vessels. This chapter explains the divine partnership between supernatural faith and natural preparation. Miracles require belief and structure.

Reflection Questions

1. Are your vessels (plans, skills, systems) big enough for what you are asking God for?
2. Where do you rely on faith but neglect preparation?

3. What practical step is God waiting for you to take?
4. How can you balance prayer and planning better?
5. What does Heaven want to release that you have not yet prepared space for?

BREAKING THE POVERTY MINDSET

"Beloved, I wish above all things that thou mayest prosper and be in health, even as thy soul prospereth." (3 John 1:2 (KJV)

Oil filled the widow's house. Vessels surrounded her. Her miracle was complete. Her debt was paid. Her future is secure.

But for many believers, the oil is not the problem. The vessels are not the problem. The instruction is not a problem. The problem is internal - a mindset formed by years of lack, shaped by seasons of struggle, inherited through generations, reinforced by culture, and strengthened by the environment.

A poverty mindset can keep a believer bound even *while standing in the middle of God's provision.*

It is possible to have oil in your house, but *lack in your mind,* to have a miracle in your hand, but *limitation in your thinking or* to receive divine supply and still *live as though you are empty.*

The Widow's Miracle Required a Renewed Mind

The widow *thought* the story of her life was over. She expected to *lose* her sons.
She anticipated *defeat*. She assumed *hardship*.

Her language revealed her mindset: "Your servant had nothing in the house…"

Yet she *did* have something. She had oil—a seed of divine potential blinded by emotional despair.

This is how poverty works: It blinds you to the possibilities in your own house.

A poverty mindset says:

"*I have nothing.*"

"*I can't change.*"

"*I don't have enough.*"

"*My life is too small.*"

"*My options are limited.*"

"*My story is finished.*"

But heaven responds: "You have oil."

Oil represents potential, gifting, wisdom, skill, creativity, resources and ability.

in the same room.

A poverty mindset interprets opportunity as risk, favor as danger, and multiplication as uncertainty.

This is why God brought her a prophet not merely to give her a miracle but change her narrative.

Your life will follow the direction of your dominant mindset. If you expect …

- decline, decline *finds you.*
- loss, it will *attach itself.*
- scarcity, you *sabotage abundance.*

But if you expect God *overflow* becomes normal.

Poverty Is Broken by Revelation, Not Money

Some people believe that giving the poor more money fixes poverty. But money given *without* mindset renewal, does not heal poverty, It often magnifies it.

Why? Poverty is a mindset rather than just a lack of financial resources, not merely a lack of financial resources. This is why many who receive financial breakthroughs return to the same patterns of scarcity: - increased income but same mindset, new opportunities but old habits, divine miracles but limited thinking.

The widow needed more than oil—She needed a new identity.

A poverty mindset cannot survive in a renewed mind.

The oil changes your environment. The Word changes your mentality.

This is why Romans 12:2 says: *"Be transformed by the renewing of your mind."*

You cannot walk in *new seasons* with old mentalities.

Signs of a Poverty Mindset

Here are some indicators that show the poverty mindset is still active:

1. Fear of using your gift: This fear stems from the belief that your gift holds no value.
2. Comfort with smallness: Because expansion feels threatening.
3. Hoarding instead of investing: You hoard because you fear that resources will never return.
4. Accepting limitations as destiny: "This is just who I am."
5. Resisting structure and discipline: Growth feels unnatural.
6. Envying others' success: Rather than gaining knowledge from it, people often envy others' achievements.
7. Think survival instead of strategy: The focus is on the present, not the future.
8. Feeling unworthy of abundance: As if prosperity is for "others."

The widow carried many of these tendencies, but the prophetic word *reshaped her mind.*

How God Breaks Poverty in a Believer's Life

God *breaks poverty* through a process:

1. Revelation—Seeing what God sees - "You have oil."
2. Instruction—Obeying divine direction - "Borrow vessels."
3. Environment—Removing limiting voices - "Shut the door."
4. Action—Doing what seems impossible - "She poured."
5. Strategy—Turning miracle into movement - "Go, sell the oil."
6. Transformation—Living in sustained abundance - "You and your sons live on the rest."

This is God's blueprint for breaking poverty: **See. Obey. Separate. Act. Strategize. Sustain.**

Each step dismantles a layer of poverty thinking and *replaces it with Kingdom identity.*

The Widow's Sons Were Saved From Poverty by Her Obedience

Poverty persists across generations. So is abundance. Your mindset will shape your family's *destiny.*

Her sons were about to inherit slavery but her renewed mind allowed them to inherit freedom. What you break in yourself is what you protect in your children.

The greatest inheritance you give your children is not money—It is a *mindset aligned with the Kingdom.*

You Cannot Hold Kingdom Oil With a Poverty Mindset

The oil represented Kingdom potential. But poverty thinking would have destroyed it.

A poverty mindset mishandles opportunity, mismanages blessing, misinterprets instruction, and miscalculates value.

You cannot walk in the kingdom of prosperity while thinking like a captive. The oil demands a renewed mind.

Your next level …is not waiting on money—It is waiting on mindset.

Summary

Poverty is not the absence of money, it is the absence of expectation, strategy, and identity. This chapter exposes the spiritual and psychological strongholds' that keep people small. True prosperity begins with renewed thinking, disciplined stewardship, and the courage to believe God for more.

Reflection Questions

1. What beliefs about money or success have limited you?
2. How has fear shaped your financial decisions?
3. What new mindset is God inviting you to adopt?
4. Where do you need discipline, not deliverance?
5. What does Kingdom prosperity look like for you?

THE CAPACITY OF VISION

"Write the vision, and make it plain upon tables, that he may run that readeth it." (Habakkuk 2:2 (KJV)

When the widow's vessels ended, The oil stopped. But the miracle did not end with oil; It transitioned into instruction and strategy.

This story forces us to confront a timeless Kingdom truth:

Oil without vision leads to stagnation.
Vision without capacity leads to frustration.
But vision with capacity leads to manifestation.

Vision is more than seeing something—It is a *divine* ability to perceive possibilities before they materialize.

Vision is the container of destiny. Without vision, *oil has no direction*. Miracles have no assignment, resources have no plan, and potential has no outlet.

Vision is capacity in picture form.

Vision Is Heaven's Blueprint for Earthly Assignment

Every miracle God provides must be interpreted through *vision*.

Oil is provision. Vision is direction.

Oil is potential. Vision is purpose.

Oil is power. Vision is focus.

In Scripture, God never gives a resource without revealing its purpose.

Noah was given wood, but also a *blueprint*.

Moses was given a staff, but also a *mission*.

David was given an anointing, but also a *kingdom*.

Esther was given favor but also an *assignment*.

Gideon was given strength but also a *strategy*.

Paul was given a revelation but also a *mandate*.

The widow was given oil, but also an *economic plan*.

Vision clarifies why the miracle came and where it is meant to take you.

Vision Is Proof of Maturity

Many pray for miracles, But God looks for vision. Vision proves readiness.

Vision reveals your seriousness, stewardship, discipline, intention, identity, preparation.

This is why Scripture says, *"Where there is no vision, the people perish"* *(Proverbs 29:18).*

Not because God abandons them, but because they cannot navigate destiny blindly.

Destiny requires sight.

Vision Determines Action

What you see determines what you do. What you believe about your future shapes how you move in your present.

Two people can have the same oil, and produce completely different outcomes, based on vision.

One sees survival. Another sees *legacy.*

One sees struggle. Another sees *opportunity.*

One sees limitation. Another sees *multiplication.*

Vision determines which vessels you gather, how far you stretch, how long you obey, how much capacity you build.

The widow gathered vessels because she believed God would fill them.

Her action revealed her vision.

Vision Expands Capacity

You *cannot grow* beyond the size of your vision.

A narrow vision creates small vessels.
A weak vision creates fragile vessels.
A fearful vision creates limited vessels.

But a Kingdom vision creates abundant vessels because it sees beyond, present pain, resources, limitations, or circumstances.

Vision gives you permission to prepare for more than what you currently see.

It was a *vision* that allowed the widow to believe that a tiny jar of oil could fill dozens of vessels.

It is vision that will allow you to believe that the little you have is enough for God to do something *extraordinary*.

Vision Requires Writing, Not Just Seeing

God told Habakkuk: "Write the vision."

Because vision is unwritten, it is unrealized.

You cannot hold a future you refuse to capture, run with a dream you refuse to articulate, build a life you cannot describe.

Writing the vision clarifies the mind, stabilizes the heart, strengthens the will, guides decisions, shapes preparation and increases faith.

Every prophetic destiny must be documented. A vision written becomes a vision actionable.

The widow may not have had scrolls, but she had instruction. Her *obedience* became her "written" vision. Her action became her documentation.

Vision Requires Alignment With Heaven

Some visions come from ambition, comparison, competition, fear, and insecurity.

But Kingdom vision comes from God.

It is birthed through prayer, submission, the Word, clarity, divine prompting, prophetic instruction and spiritual alignment.

The widow's vision *did not come from imagination.* It came from instruction.

Her vision was not self-made—It was heaven-breathed.

God-centered vision produces supernatural results.

Vision Must Mature Into Strategy

Vision *without a plan* is simply imagination.

The widow's vision matured into strategy:

- borrow vessels (capacity)
- shut the door (environment).
- pour the oil (action).

- fill the vessels (consistency).
- sell the oil (economics)
- pay the debt (freedom)
- live on the rest (sustainability)

This was not a miracle alone. It was a **business model,** a **life strategy**, and a **kingdom blueprint**.

Vision matures when it becomes executable.

Vision is seeing. Strategy is doing.

Vision shows you the mountain. Strategy gives you the steps.

Vision Defines the Future of Your Oil

Every gift God gives you is tied to a vision.

Your oil—your calling, gifting, skill, grace was never meant to exist without direction.

A visionless gift becomes wasted potential. A vision-filled gift becomes Kingdom impact.

Your oil is *not* for entertainment, survival, or applause.

Your oil *is* for the assignment, for impact, for transformation, for building, and for change.

Vision gives your will its divine target.

When Vision Expands, Life Expands

The widow's life expanded because her vision expanded.

She saw beyond her grief, debt, pain, past, and limitations.

She saw the possibility of pouring, filling, selling, living, or thriving.

Vision transformed her identity before it *transformed her economy.* Vision made her see herself differently, her oil differently, and her future differently.

When vision changes, everything changes.

Summary

Vision expands capacity. What you see determines what you build. The widow's obedience opened her eyes to possibilities she never imagined. Vision gives direction, boundaries, passion, and endurance. Without vision, vessels remain empty; with vision, they become containers for destiny.

Reflection Questions

1. What is your current vision for your life or ministry?
2. How big is your vision compared to your calling?
3. What do you need to clarify, write, or refine?
4. Who can help you sharpen your vision?
5. How does your daily life align with your God-given vision

PREPARING FOR THE OIL OF TOMORROW

"Go, sell the oil and pay your debts; you and your sons can live on the rest." (2 Kings 4:7 (ESV)

God never performs a miracle for a single moment. He performs miracles with tomorrow in mind.

The widow's oil was not just a crisis intervention. It was a future preservation plan.

Her sons were spared, debt was canceled, home was secure and her livelihood was restored.

But the most powerful part of this story is found in the last phrase: "…you and your sons can live on the rest."

This is *more* than survival language. This is generational vision language.

It means:

You will not *return* to poverty, *revisit* the same bondage, *repeat* this crisis.

Your sons will never know this level of fear again.

Your future is protected by the strategy God has given you.

Today's oil must prepare you for the oil of tomorrow.

Yesterday's Oil Is Not Enough for Tomorrow's Assignment

Just because the vessels are full today *does not mean* your preparation is complete.

Every new season of life requires a new level of preparation.

The widow received a miracle, but that *miracle came with responsibility*.

What she did *after* the miracle determined the future of her house.

The same is true for every believer: The oil God releases today must be stewarded in such a way that it brings stability, strategy, and strength for tomorrow.

Oil without preparation becomes *waste*. Oil *with preparation* becomes legacy.

Tomorrow's Oil Requires Today's Wisdom

The widow's future depended on two things:

1. The oil she already received
2. The decisions she made after receiving it

It was not enough to have oil, she needed wisdom, discipline, and planning.

Many believers *lose tomorrow's blessings* because they mishandle today's oil.

God gives miracles but, He expects stewardship.

He gives opportunity. but expects structure.

He gives resources but expects responsibility.

This is why Scripture says: *A wise man stores up treasure.* (Proverbs 21:20)

The widow was instructed to live on the rest, which means she had to budget the blessing.

For the first time in a long time, she had not only provision, but options.

Tomorrow's oil demands maturity.

Preparing for Tomorrow Means Thinking Beyond Crisis

Before the widow's encounter with Elisha, Her entire life was reactive.

She was reacting to debt, fear, loss, and pressure

Miracles change your mindset from *reactive* to proactive.

God delivered her from crisis so she could begin thinking about the future.

A poverty mindset thinks about survival. A kingdom mindset thinks about strategy.

Crisis thinking asks: *"What do I do now?"*

Kingdom thinking asks: *"What am I building for later?"*

Preparing for the oil of tomorrow requires shifting your thinking beyond emergencies and into expectation.

The Oil of Tomorrow Requires Systems

She was now operating a miracle-based business. Her home had become her *oil-distribution center.*

But the future cannot be sustained without systems.

She needed discipline in her daily rhythms, structure in how she sold the oil, consistency in managing the income, organization in handling her household, planning for her sons' future, clarity on how to manage seasons of plenty.

Many believers want miracles but resist systems.

Yet the Kingdom grows on order, stewardship, discipline, and consistency.

Even the miracle of multiplication stopped when the system reached its limit.

Preparation requires more vessels. not just physically, but structurally.

Prepare Before You Need More Oil

One of the greatest secrets of Kingdom living is this: Prepare in peace for what you will need in pressure.

Those who wait for pressure to build capacity are *always late.*

The widow's miracle ended, but her responsibility began.

God gave her *enough oil* for today and enough wisdom for tomorrow.

The believer who prepares *avoids* unnecessary crises, *manages* seasons with clarity, *anticipates* needs before they arise, *grows* without stress, *builds* without fear.

Preparation is not a lack of faith. Preparation is the fruit of faith.

Joseph *saved Egypt* because he prepared during abundance.

Noah *saved humanity* because he prepared during calm.

Esther *saved* Israel because she prepared in private.

David *ruled* well because he prepared in obscurity.

Jesus *prepared* 30 years for a 3½-year ministry.

Great destinies are always attached to great preparation.

Tomorrow's Oil Requires Protecting Today's Oil

Preparation also means protection.

The widow went from nothing to abundance.

With abundance comes responsibility namely, protecting her miracle, guarding her household, shielding her sons from bondage, stewarding her business, defending her peace, maintaining boundaries, and staying aligned with God's instruction.

The enemy often returns after a miracle to test whether the believer understands stewardship.

Her sons were once targeted to become slaves. Now the responsibility was to ensure they *never faced that danger again.*

Preparing for tomorrow means safeguarding the blessing of today.

Tomorrow Belongs to Those Who Steward Today

God *did not simply save the widow.* He shifted her from panic to planning, fear to foresight, survival to strategy, desperation to discipline.

"Live on the rest." is a kingdom command!

It means to regulate your life around God's provision, build your future intentionally, sustain what God has given you, create margin position your children for stability, preserve the blessing and think generationally.

The oil was a provision for the moment. Her decisions would

determine her next decade.

Preparing for Tomorrow's Oil in Your Own Life

This chapter is not just about the widow—It is about you.

God is preparing you for greater assignments, deeper purpose, larger responsibilities, wider influence, increased ministry, elevated platforms, higher levels of stewardship.

But increase without preparation leads to *collapse.*

Tomorrow's oil requires a renewed mind, growing discipline, expanded capacity, clearer vision, stronger structure, deeper consecration, wiser habits, strategic planning, and consistent prayer.

God is not only pouring oil into your life—He is preparing you to carry more.

Summary

Capacity is not only about today; it prepares you for future oil. This chapter emphasizes anticipation, foresight, planning, and readiness. Tomorrow's opportunities require today's development. Those who build systems early receive more when the appointed time arrives.

Reflection Questions

1. What future assignment are you preparing for now?
2. What skills or habits must you develop for your next season?
3. Are you building systems that will sustain future increase?
4. How do you need to expand your "vessel" for tomorrow's oil?

5. What does long-term obedience look like for you?

FAITH + CAPACITY IN MINISTRY, MARRIAGE, MONEY, AND LEADERSHIP

"Through wisdom a house is built, and by understanding it is established; by knowledge the rooms are filled with all precious and pleasant riches." (Proverbs 24:3–4 (NKJV)

Faith is the divine force that *connects you to God's power*. Capacity is the human discipline that shapes what that power can achieve through you.

Faith without capacity creates *frustration*. Capacity without faith creates *limitation*. But faith and capacity together create transformation.

Every area of life demands both!

Your anointing flows through the vessels in your structure. Your gift flows through the vessel of your maturity, and your calling flows through the vessel of your stewardship.

This chapter explores how the widow's story applies to the four realms where believers struggle most—but also where God desires to shine most: ministry, marriage, money, and leadership.

Because God's will is never just that you survive in these spheres— His will is that you excel, multiply, and manifest the Kingdom in each one.

Capacity Determines What Heaven Can Trust You With.

1. ***Faith and Capacity in Ministry***

Many people enter ministry with passion but not enough preparation. Zeal without structure leads to burnout. Anointing without boundaries leads to exhaustion. Calling without development leads to stagnation.

The widow teaches us that God may give oil, but He still requires:

- vessels (systems),
- sons (teams),
- instructions (order),
- doors shut (consecration),
- selling (execution),
- living (sustainability).

Ministry is not sustained by pure gifting; it is sustained by:

- prayer + planning
- revelation + structure
- spirit + strategy
- anointing + administration
- passion + process

The myth that "God will do it all" is *not biblical.*

God gives the oil. You *build the vessels.*

God gives the vision. You *build the structure.*

God gives the people. You *develop leadership.*

God gives the breakthrough. You *steward the result.*

A pastor can have miracles yet lose momentum WITHOUT systems.

A leader can *preach with fire yet* lack fruit without follow-through.

A church can *have anointing but* fail to grow without administration.

This is why Acts 6 had to appoint deacons because miracles require management.

2. **Faith and Capacity in Marriage**

Marriage is a vessel—one of the most sacred, delicate, and spiritually charged vessels in the Kingdom.

Many marriages fail not because they lack love, but because they lack capacity.

Oil alone cannot save a marriage.

You need:

- *communication* capacity,

- *forgiveness* capacity,
- *emotional* capacity,
- *maturity* capacity,
- *listening* capacity,
- *conflict-resolution* capacity,
- *spiritual* capacity,
- *humility* capacity.

Just as the widow had to shut the door for the oil to flow, marriage requires private obedience. Including private prayer together, accountability, healing, honesty, and work.

God can pour love into a marriage, but if the vessels are small, the *flow will be limited.*

Marriage demands both faith and skill.

Faith to believe God for your spouse.

Capacity to become the spouse God wants you to be.

Faith to weather storms.

Capacity to resolve them with wisdom.

Faith to pray together.

Capacity to communicate respectfully.

Marriage collapses when one spouse has faith but no capacity, or capacity but *no faith.*

The miracle of a thriving marriage is always born through both.

3. ***Faith + Capacity in Money***

Money is one of the clearest realms where the widow's story becomes a blueprint.

She had oil but without vessels, She remained broke.

She had a miracle but without a plan, Her sons would become slaves.

She had provision but without strategy, She could not step into prosperity.

God multiplied her oil. But the prophet told her to: "…sell the oil… pay the debt… live on the rest."

This is the template for Kingdom economics:

Miracle → divine supply

Selling → marketplace engagement

Paying debt → financial freedom

Living on the rest → sustainability and management

Many believers have faith for money but no capacity for money.

They pray for increase but have no plan.

They shout for a breakthrough but avoid budgeting.

They declare abundance but resist discipline.

They expect overflow while maintaining leaky vessels.

God gives seed. You create the storehouse.

The enemy uses two strategies to keep generations in *financial bondage*:

Lack of faith

Lack of stewardship

The widow conquered both.

Her faith accessed' the miracle and her capacity created stability.

4.   **Faith and Capacity in Leadership**

Leadership is the *ultimate vessel*. Everything God will do through your life must *flow through your leadership capacity.*

Leadership is not a title—It is a *container.*

Anointing does not make you a leader.

Assignments do not make you a leader.

Followers do not make you a leader.

CAPACITY MAKES YOU A LEADER!

In leadership, faith is essential: faith to see what others cannot see, move when others stand still and to believe when others doubt.

But faith alone is not enough.

Leadership requires vision, discipline, emotional intelligence, decision-making, wisdom, boundaries, consistency, humility, growth and accountability.

A leader must have a large internal vessel because God sends people according to the size of your heart.

A leader must carry more than others …

endure more than others,

see farther than others,

and sacrifice more than others.

The widow teaches us that leadership is not about being strong. It is about being prepared.

Weak leaders do not fail for lack of oil. They fail for lack of vessels.

Leaders fall when the assignment outgrows their container. But leaders thrive. when their capacity meets their calling.

When Faith and Capacity Unite, Transformation Happens

These four areas, namely, *ministry, marriage, money, and leadership* represent the pillars of a whole life.

Your *assignment* demands faith. Your destiny demands capacity.

Faith gives you access. Capacity gives you expression.

Faith opens heaven. Capacity builds earth.

Faith reaches upward. Capacity spreads outward.

Faith attracts blessing. Capacity sustains blessing.

The widow's miracle shows us what every believer must embrace: God will pour more oil when you prepare more vessels.

Summary

This chapter applies the principles of capacity to real-life areas: ministry, marriage, finances, and leadership. Faith opens the door, but capacity determines success in relationships, stewardship, influence, and calling. Every area thrives when faith and preparation work together.

Reflection Questions

1. Which area of your life needs increased capacity now?
2. How do you balance faith and planning in practical matters?
3. What relational habits need to improve to support your growth?
4. What leadership capacity must you develop this year?
5. How can you better steward your marriage, ministry, or finances?

LIVING A LIFE GOD CAN FILL

"Blessed are those who hunger and thirst for righteousness, for they shall be filled." (Matthew 5:6 (NKJV)

A miracle-filled life is not reserved for a spiritual elite. It is not a privilege for prophets, pastors, or patriarchs. It is the inheritance of every believer who chooses to live as a vessel God can continually fill.

The widow was **not** extraordinary in her status. She was not wealthy, influential, or highly positioned.

She was *simply* available. She was willing, obedient, desperate enough to listen, humble enough to learn, and courageous enough to act.

God *does not fill perfect vessels.* — He fills prepared ones.

To live a life that God can fill is to live a life that stays open, surrendered, and aligned with heaven's rhythm.

The Secret of a Life God Can Fill

The widow teaches us the spiritual posture required for continual filling. God filled her vessels, not because she was special, but because she was positioned.

A life God can fill has three core postures:

1. **Posture of Surrender** - "What do you have in your house?"

She surrendered what she had even though she thought it was *insignificant.*

God fills surrendered vessels not self-sufficient ones.

2. **Posture of Obedience** - "Go, borrow vessels…"

She obeyed without analyzing, debating, or delaying.

Obedience is the funnel through which the oil flows.

3. **Posture of Faith** - "She poured…"

She *acted* on what seemed foolish. And God honored her action.

Faith is the catalyst of divine movement.

These three postures include surrender, obedience, and faith.

These create the life God is eager to fill.

Living with Holy Expectation

To live a life God can fill, You must live with expectation.

Expectation is not passive hope— It is *spiritual readiness*.

People who expect God to fill them pray differently, think differently, plan differently, prepare differently, speak differently, and act differently.

Expectation enlarges your internal vessel. It pulls the *future* into the present. It *draws* the supernatural toward you. Expectation is the *spiritual magnet* of the Kingdom.

Living a Life of Continual Capacity

The widow gathered enough vessels for one miracle. But you must learn to gather vessels, for a lifetime.

A life God can fill is a life of consistent prayer, surrender, growth, holiness, obedience, preparation, learning.

God does not pour into people who are occasionally hungry. He pours into those who live in pursuit. *"He satisfies the longing soul."* (Psalm 107:9)

The deeper your hunger, the greater your capacity.

Living a Life of Private Integrity

The instruction was, Shut the door." It was not *just a moment*; it was a model.

Behind that door, the widow *experienced transformation.* Behind that door, the *oil multiplied*.

Behind that door, a *strategy was born.*
Behind that door, *destiny shifted.*

A life God *can fill* is a life of private integrity.

God fills you in the secret place before He uses you in the public place.

He pours in *quiet seasons,* in *hidden* places, in *unseen* moments.

If your private life is empty, Your *public life will eventually leak.*

People *admire* public miracles, but God admires private obedience.

Living a Life of Divine Alignment

When the widow aligned her life with the prophetic instruction, everything shifted. Divine alignment is the freeway of the supernatural.

Alignment means, your …

- thoughts align with God's Word.
- choices align with God's ways.
- priorities align with God's agenda.
- values align with Kingdom culture.
- relationships align with your assignment.
- environment aligns with your purpose.

God cannot fill you if your life is filled with distractions, compromise, unbelief, and divided loyalty.

The filling of God requires room. Capacity requires space. Oil requires emptiness.

Empty vessels are vessels that have made room for God.

Living a Life of Stewardship

After the *miracle,* the widow had to steward the oil. Stewardship is not what you do, when you have nothing. It is what you do, when God has given you something.

A life God can fill is a life that:

- honor what God gives.
- protects what God gives
- multiplies what God gives
- manages what God gives.
- appreciate what God gives.

You prepare your future, by *stewarding* your present, and God will continue to fill what you *continually honor.*

Living a Life of Generational Vision

When God filled the widow's vessels, He was not only thinking about her, but He was also thinking about her sons, their children, and the legacy that would follow.

A life God can fill is a life lived with generational consciousness.

This means, you think beyond yourself, act with tomorrow in mind, and build for those who will come after you.

The widow's obedience saved her children from slavery and opened the door to *generational* stability.

When God fills you, He fills your *house,* your *lineage,* your future. God pours into people who understand the weight of legacy.

You Were Created to Be filled.

Every chapter of the widow's journey reveals a GREATER KINGDOM truth:

You were created to be a vessel God can fill.

A vessel of oil, purpose, destiny, wisdom, faith, revelation, obedience, influence, grace, excellence and impact.

The question is not *whether God wants to fill you*, the question is whether your life is shaped in a way that *He can.*

You are not random, empty by accident, overlooked, or forgotten.

You are a vessel—*chosen*, *crafted*, *designed*—not to remain empty, but to carry the fullness of God.

Your assignment is simple: Live a life God can fill, and He will fill it, again and again, and again.

Summary

God fills what is available, surrendered, and properly positioned. This chapter teaches that capacity is not accidental—it is cultivated through humility, obedience, purity, and intentionality. A life aligned with God's rhythm becomes a vessel Heaven can trust. When your posture is right, the oil flows naturally.

Reflection Questions

1. What areas of your life need more surrender?
2. How can you position yourself daily to receive more from God?
3. What habits make your vessel "fillable"?
4. What attitudes or distractions might be blocking the flow?
5. How does obedience enlarge your spiritual capacity?

CONCLUSION

WHEN FAITH MEETS CAPACITY

"According to your faith be it unto you." (Matthew 9:29)
"Make this valley full of ditches." (2 Kings 3:16)

Every chapter of this book has traced the sacred dance between what Heaven provides and what earth prepares.

The widow's story is more than a miracle account it is a prophetic blueprint for every believer who desires to step into fullness, multiplication, and destiny.

Her life teaches us that:

- faith opens the door,
- obedience walks through it,
- capacity sustains what obedience received,
- and wisdom builds a future from what faith accessed.

This is the divine equation of Kingdom increase.

Your life rises at the intersection of two forces: God's power and your preparation.

Oil without vessels stops flowing.

Vision without structure stagnates.

Calling without character collapses.

Miracles without management evaporate.

Purpose without discipline never matures.

But when faith meets capacity, everything changes.

You Are the Vessel God Chose

If there is one truth you must carry beyond this book, it is this:

You are the vessel. You are the house. You are the container God wants to fill.

God is not looking for the perfect. He is looking for the prepared.

He is not looking for the strong. He is looking for the surrendered.

He is not looking for the flawless. He is looking for the available.

Like the widow, you may have underestimated what is in your house your gift, your story, your potential, your wisdom, your grace.

But God sees oil where you see emptiness. He sees purpose where you see pain. He sees calling where you see crisis. He sees future where you see fear.

You are not empty. You are equipped.

You are not forgotten. You are positioned.

You are not overlooked. You are chosen.

Your Miracle Begins With What You Have

The widow discovered that her breakthrough was never outside her home. It was already inside her house— waiting for recognition, activation, and obedience.

The same is true of you.

Your life already contains:

- the seed of your next level,
- the idea that will shift your future,
- the gift that will open doors,
- the wisdom shaped through your pain,
- the oil hidden in your story.

You do not need more oil. You need more capacity to contain what God wants to pour.

Your Future Requires New Vessels

If you have learned anything through these pages, let it be this:

Miracles do not happen according to need. They happen according to capacity.

Every breakthrough in your life will require you to:

- stretch,
- enlarge,
- borrow vessels,

- shut wrong doors,
- pour faithfully,
- protect your environment,
- build systems,
- break old mindsets,
- develop new disciplines,
- prepare for the future.

Your next level will not come to the person you are today—it will come to the person you are becoming.

The oil of tomorrow will demand greater faith, greater structure, greater vision, greater integrity and greater stewardship.

You cannot step into the next dimension with yesterday's containers.

God Has More Oil Than You Have Vessels

This truth should humble you, strengthen you, and ignite you.

Heaven is not struggling to bless you. God is not rationing miracles. The Holy Spirit is not withholding increase. The limitation is not above you—it is within you.

But the good news is this:

- Capacity can grow.
- Vessels can increase.
- Mindsets can change.

- Systems can be built.
- Vision can expand.
- Discipline can develop.
- Faith can mature.

You are not stuck. You are simply being invited into expansion.

Your Life Is About to Overflow

The widow began her story in despair. She ended it in overflow.

She began grieving. She ended thriving.

She began to be afraid for her children She ended securing their future.

Her house, that once echoed with emptiness, became a factory of abundance.

Her cry for help became her testimony of provision.

This is what happens when faith meets capacity.

THIS IS YOUR INVITATION

As you close this book, you are stepping into a new beginning.

God is calling you to:

- discover your oil,
- expand your vessels,
- borrow wisely,
- shut doors strategically,
- pour with obedience,
- build systems for increase,
- break limiting mindsets,
- live a life He can continually fill.

This is not the end of a reading experience. It is the beginning of a transformation journey.

Your miracle is not a moment. Your miracle is a lifestyle.

Your life is not a random jar. Your life is a *vessel* of divine purpose.

And your future is not limited by your past—it is limited only by your preparation.

Now is the time to believe boldly.

Now is the time to prepare relentlessly.

Now is the time to enlarge your capacity.

Now is the time to embrace overflow.

Because when faith meets capacity—destiny comes alive.

[FINAL PROPHETIC SEAL]
May your vessels multiply.
May your oil never cease.
May your faith rise.
May your capacity expand.
And may your life become
a testimony of God's endless supply.

21-DAY ACTIVATION GUIDE

DAY 1 — *Acknowledge Your Crisis Honestly*

Scripture: 2 Kings 4:1
Focus: Transformation begins when you stop pretending you are okay.
Prophetic Insight: God meets you at the level of your honesty.
Action: Write down the crisis you want God to transform.
Prayer: *Lord, I bring my reality before You. Meet me in truth and awaken my faith.*

DAY 2 — *Ask the Two Destiny Questions*

Scripture: 2 Kings 4:2
Focus: Clarity is the gateway to miracles.
Prophetic Insight: Heaven responds to clear requests.
Action: Answer in writing: *What do I want God to do? What do I have?*
Prayer: *Give me clarity, Lord. Show me what is already in my house.*

DAY 3 — *Recognize Your Hidden "BUT"*

Scripture: 2 Kings 4:2b
Focus: Your "but" is the pivot from lack to faith.
Prophetic Insight: You are not empty—you are unaware.
Action: Identify an overlooked gift or asset.
Prayer: *Open my eyes to what I have dismissed or minimized.*

DAY 4 — *Identify Your Oil*

Scripture: 1 Peter 4:10
Focus: Your gift is your oil.
Prophetic Insight: God multiplies what you recognize.
Action: List three strengths or abilities people often affirm in you.
Prayer: *Reveal my oil and give me courage to value it.*

DAY 5 — *Confront the Poverty Mindset*

Scripture: Romans 12:2
Focus: Poverty is first a mindset, not a wallet.
Prophetic Insight: God cannot fill what fear keeps empty.
Action: Write one limiting belief and replace it with truth.
Prayer: *Renew my mind, Lord. Break every small way of thinking.*

DAY 6 — *Ask for Help Without Shame*

Scripture: 2 Kings 4:3
Focus: Borrowing requires humility.
Prophetic Insight: Increase is often hidden in community.
Action: Ask someone for wisdom, help, or mentorship.
Prayer: *Give me humility to grow through others.*

DAY 7 — *Borrow Vessels Widely*

Scripture: Proverbs 11:14
Focus: Expansion requires diverse voices.
Prophetic Insight: Your miracle will often come from unexpected connections.
Action: Reach out to someone outside your comfort zone.
Prayer: *Expand my relational circle with wisdom and favor.*

DAY 8 — *Protect Your Process (Shut the Door)*

Scripture: 2 Kings 4:4
Focus: What God is doing in you requires privacy.
Prophetic Insight: Some rooms birth miracles; others kill them.
Action: Identify one distraction to eliminate.
Prayer: *Help me guard the sacred work You are doing in me.*

DAY 9 — *Start Pouring in Faith*

Scripture: James 2:17
Focus: Faith becomes real when action begins.
Prophetic Insight: God multiplies movement, not intentions.
Action: Begin the first small step toward a dream.
Prayer: *Lord, I pour in faith. Multiply what I offer You.*

DAY 10 — *Honor the Law of Process*

Scripture: Ecclesiastes 3:1
Focus: Pouring happens one vessel at a time.
Prophetic Insight: God multiplies consistency.
Action: Choose one area to be faithfully consistent in for the next 7 days.
Prayer: *Make me faithful in the process, not frustrated.*

DAY 11 — *Expand Your Vision*

Scripture: Habakkuk 2:2
Focus: Vision is capacity.
Prophetic Insight: You cannot hold what you cannot see.
Action: Write or rewrite your vision clearly.
Prayer: *Enlarge my inner sight, Lord.*

DAY 12 — Break the Limitation of Few Vessels

Scripture: Isaiah 54:2
Focus: Stop limiting your future based on your past.
Prophetic Insight: God's oil is bigger than your imagination.
Action: Identify one limiting pattern and stretch beyond it.
Prayer: *Father, enlarge me within. Increase my capacity.*

DAY 13 — Build Systems for Future Oil

Scripture: Luke 14:28
Focus: Systems sustain miracles.
Prophetic Insight: Structure is the womb of increase.
Action: Build or refine one system (budget, schedule, prayer routine).
Prayer: *Give me wisdom to build what supports my destiny.*

DAY 14 — Defend Your Environment

Scripture: Proverbs 4:23
Focus: Protect your atmosphere—emotionally, spiritually, relationally.
Prophetic Insight: Oil flows where peace reigns.
Action: Remove one toxic influence.
Prayer: *Guard my space, Lord, and lead me into peace.*

DAY 15 — Steward the Oil

Scripture: Luke 16:10
Focus: What you manage grows.
Prophetic Insight: Stewardship attracts supernatural flow.
Action: Allocate time or resources intentionally.
Prayer: *Teach me to steward increase with wisdom.*

DAY 16 — Monetize the Oil ("Sell the Oil")

Scripture: Deuteronomy 8:18
Focus: Your gift carries economic power.
Prophetic Insight: Your oil can fund your life and assignment.
Action: Identify one way your gift can serve others profitably.
Prayer: *Give me ideas and courage to activate wealth through my gift.*

DAY 17 — Live on the Rest (Build Longevity)

Scripture: Proverbs 21:20
Focus: Sustainability matters as much as breakthrough.
Prophetic Insight: God wants you blessed for the long haul.
Action: Create a plan to sustain growth (savings, habits, relationships).
Prayer: *Establish me, Lord, in long-term increase.*

DAY 18 — Honor Your Mentors and Borrowed Vessels

Scripture: Hebrews 13:7
Focus: Relationships carry spiritual weight.
Prophetic Insight: Honor keeps doors open.
Action: Thank someone who poured into you.
Prayer: *Give me a spirit of honor that unlocks future vessels.*

DAY 19 — Live as a Vessel God Can Fill

Scripture: Matthew 5:6
Focus: Hunger determines capacity.
Prophetic Insight: God fills the thirsty.
Action: Schedule dedicated time to seek God deeply today.
Prayer: *Fill me, Lord. Make me a vessel ready for You.*

DAY 20 — *Prepare for Tomorrow's Oil*

Scripture: 1 Corinthians 2:9
Focus: God has already planned your next level.
Prophetic Insight: Preparation is proof of expectation.
Action: Prepare one thing that your future self will need.
Prayer: *Equip me for the future You designed.*

DAY 21 — *Declare Overflow Over Your Life*

Scripture: Psalm 23:5
Focus: Overflow is your Kingdom heritage.
Prophetic Insight: God never intended you to live in barely enough.
Action: Write a prophetic declaration for your next 12 months.
Prayer:
My cup runs over.
My vessels increase.
My oil will never stop.
My life is rising.
My future is expanding.
My purpose is unfolding.
In Jesus' name. Amen.

www.ingramcontent.com/pod-product-compliance
Lightning Source LLC
Chambersburg PA
CBHW052220090526
44585CB00015BA/1261